Amsterdam City Guide, Netherlands

Holland Travel

Author
Thomas Bailey

Publisher:
SONIT
2162 Davenport House, 261 Bolton Road. Bury. Lancashire. BL8 2NZ. United Kingdom

Table of Content

Summary

Traveling and Tourism

Tourism is a global industry, which involves people travelling across the world for a variety of reasons mainly recreation and sightseeing. When tourists decide where to travel, they often base their decisions on the attractions and situations in a city or country. Sometimes countries are in the midst of political unrest, such as war, civil war or terrorism. Tourists will avoid these destinations, choosing more peaceful destinations instead. However, while they are there, unforeseen situations may occur, such as tsunamis, natural disasters, diseases or accidents. It is important for tourism professionals and for tourists themselves to adequately prepare, through thorough research, before they (or their clients) leave on a journey.

Every country has sights of attractions and places of interest, some of which are not known that easy, and to discover them, you have to need a guide on the interested place, learn about local people's attitude and relation with foreginers, it is important to know all these. This is the importance of Tourist Book Guide.

Indroduction

Amsterdam, city and port, western Netherlands, located on the IJsselmeer and connected to the North Sea. It is the capital and the principal commercial and financial centre of the Netherlands.

To the scores of tourists who visit each year, Amsterdam is known for its historical attractions, for its collections of great art, and for the distinctive colour and flavour of its old sections, which have been so well preserved. However, visitors to the city also see a crowded metropolis beset by environmental pollution, traffic congestion, and housing shortages. It is easy to describe Amsterdam, which is more than 700 years old, as a living museum of a bygone age and to praise the eternal beauty of the centuries-old canals, the ancient patrician houses, and the atmosphere of freedom and tolerance, but the modern city is still working out solutions to the pressing urban problems that confront it.

Amsterdam is the nominal capital of the Netherlands but not the seat of government, which is The Hague. The royal family, for example, is only occasionally in residence at the Royal Palace, on the square known as the Dam, in Amsterdam. The city lacks the monumental architecture found in other capitals. There are no wide squares suitable for big parades, nor are there triumphal arches or imposing statues. Amsterdam's intimate character is best reflected in the narrow, bustling streets of the old town, where much of the population still goes about its business. While there are reminders of the glorious past gabled houses, noble brick facades clad with sandstone, richly decorated cornices, towers and churches, and the music of carillons and barrel organs the realities of life in the modern city often belie this romantic image.

The inner city is divided by its network of canals into some 90 "islands," and the municipality contains approximately 1,300 bridges and viaducts. Amsterdam is the economic centre of the Netherlands, and there tradition persists alongside innovation. Although the city has a modern metro system, about one-fifth of the workforce still relies on the time-honoured bicycle for transportation. The city continues to be famous for its countless Chinese and Indonesian restaurants and the hundreds of houseboats that line its canals. Since the mid-1960s Amsterdam also has been known for a permissive atmosphere, and it attracts many people seeking an alternative lifestyle. Area city, 64 square miles (165 square km); metro. area, 245 square miles (635 square km). Pop. (2008 est.) city, 1,028,603; metro. area, 1,482,676.

Physical and Human Geography

The landscape
The city layout
Amsterdam is situated in a flat and low-lying area mainly on the south bank of the IJ, an inland arm of the

former Zuiderzee, now the IJsselmeer, connected by canal with the North Sea. The Amstel River flows from south to north through the city toward the IJ. Parts of the city lie below sea level, some of them on land that has been reclaimed from the sea or from marshes or lakes.

City development

The current Dutch capital first took shape as a small medieval settlement on dikes containing the Amstel where it met the IJ. The Amstel was dammed to control flooding, and the city's name derives from the Amstel dam. By the 16th century Amsterdam had grown into a walled city centred on the present Dam, bounded approximately by what are now the Singel and the Kloveniersburgwal canals. Three towers of the old fortifications still stand. Outside the Singel are the three main canals dating from the early 17th century: the Herengracht (Gentlemen's Canal), Keizersgracht (Emperor's Canal), and Prinsengracht (Prince's Canal). These concentric canals, together with the smaller radial canals, form a characteristic spiderweb pattern, which was extended east along the harbour and west into the district known as the Jordaan during the prosperous Golden Age (the 17th and early 18th centuries).

The old part of Amsterdam has many ancient buildings, most notably the Old Church (Oude Kerk), built in the 13th century, and the New Church (Nieuwe Kerk), begun in the 15th century. Next to the New Church is the 17th-century city hall, now the Royal Palace, built in classical Palladian style. Other significant buildings include the Mint Tower (Munttoren), with a 17th-century spire resting on a medieval gate; the South Church (Zuiderkerk, 1611); the West Church (Westerkerk, 1631), where Rembrandt is buried; the Trippenhuis, housing the Royal Netherlands Academy of Arts and Sciences; and the Old Man's House Gate (Oudemanhuispoort), now the entrance to one of the University of Amsterdam's main buildings. The former Jewish quarter, in the eastern portion of the old town, is the location of the Portuguese Synagogue (1671) and the Rembrandt House (Rembrandthuis), which is now a museum. The old town's three main squares are the Dam, the Leidseplein (Leiden Square), and the Rembrandtplein (Rembrandt Square). Fine 17th- and 18th-century patrician houses line the canals.

Major physical change came again to the cityscape in the late 19th and early 20th centuries, when the booming colonial trade fueled industrialization and the expansion of the city's population. For example, new inexpensive residential, commercial, and industrial construction filled De Pijp, a neighbourhood in the southern part of the city, and workers crowded into the older buildings of the Jordaan in the west. The North Sea Canal, a major new channel running west to the sea, was completed in 1876; new docks and warehouses developed along the waterfront; and in 1889 the city's new rail hub, Central Station, was built on an artificial island in the IJ north of the city centre. In the early 20th century new suburbs were built, several in the Amsterdam school of architectural style; their imaginative, asymmetrical motifs broke up the monotony associated with suburban public housing units. Sint Nicolaas Church (1886), the Beurs (Stock Exchange; 1903), and the Shipping House (1916) date from this period, as do the Rijksmuseum (1876–85), the Concertgebouw (Concert Hall; 1888), the Stedelijk Museum (1895), the Olympic Stadium (1928), and the Amstel Station (1939).

Amsterdam suffered less damage than many other European cities during World War II, but the old Jewish quarter was razed. After the war, urban renewal programs and large-scale new housing estates attempted to accommodate increasing population, rising incomes, and the inexorable growth in automobile traffic. New garden suburbs included Slotermeer on the western edge of the city, Nieuwendam in the north, Buitenveldert in the south, and, in the 1970s, Bijlmermeer in the southeast. Bijlmermeer was the ultimate in modernist utopian urban planning, with bicycle paths, playgrounds, and high-rises built along the city's new metro line. However, it was not a success and was later partly demolished and redeveloped in a mix of building styles for a variety of uses. Since the 1970s, low-rise mixed housing projects have been the vogue, including both public housing and private-sector dwellings. Recent developments of this kind have been built in Sloten and the Middelveldsche Akerpolder in the west, while in the east, in the old harbour district, intense housing construction began in the 1990s. During the last decades of the 20th century, inner-city areas were increasingly renovated rather than replaced.

The people

Amsterdam is a small city compared with most national capitals. After World War II the population stood at more than 800,000; it declined until the mid-1980s but has generally risen since then. Recent increases are due to a steady surplus of births over deaths and to an influx of immigrants. About half of the city's inhabitants are indigenous Dutch; about one-tenth are of Surinamese origin; and there are significant Moroccan and Turkish minorities. Amsterdam has been a home to immigrants since the 16th century. More recently, many have come from the former Dutch empire (Indonesia, Suriname, and the islands of the former Netherlands Antilles). Others have come as "guest workers," especially from Morocco and Turkey, or as employees of multinational corporations and students from developed countries. Moreover, during the 1990s many new immigrants came as asylum seekers. Non-European minorities now comprise well over one-third of Amsterdam's population (and about two-thirds of those less than 19 years old), and the city has an active policy of integration, based on language learning and social orientation.

The birth and marriage rates have been rising since the mid-1990s. Meanwhile, as in other Western societies, increasing numbers live alone, in single-parent families, or as unmarried couples. Unlike the population of the Netherlands as a whole, that of Amsterdam has not become older demographically. Pre-retirement-age residents are not a shrinking share of the population, mainly because there is a continual influx of younger people.

The economy

Like most modern cities, Amsterdam is a service centre, with only about one-tenth of its workforce employed in manufacturing. The most vibrant and expanding part of the dominant service sector is its business services component, including consulting, information and medical technology, and telecommunications. The consistent lifeblood of the city for the past seven centuries has been international trade and transport, which together account for about one-fifth of employment. Banking and insurance also have been a mainstay of the Amsterdam economy, together accounting for about one-eighth of all jobs, while about one-sixth of jobholders are employed in health, cultural, and social services. Another important part of the city's economy, tourism, accounts for about one-tenth of all jobs. However, despite this thriving service sector, at the turn of the 21st century the city had many job seekers who lacked marketable skills, and about one-eighth of the workforce was unemployed.

Finance and trade

Amsterdam is a very popular location for international business, mainly because of its combination of accessibility, cultural richness, cosmopolitan character, and a human scale that results from the absence of high-rise buildings and multilane highways. The Netherlands has attracted no less than one-fifth of all U.S. and Japanese investment in Europe, and much of this is focused on Amsterdam. The city also is a major financial centre, though a less important one than London or Frankfurt. All major Dutch banks have their headquarters in the city, as do the European Options Exchange and the Dutch branch of the Euronext

Securities Exchange, and some 60 foreign banks have offices there. The city's busy port and excellent land and air transportation links have allowed it to maintain its importance as a centre for regional and international trade.

Industry

Industry no longer accounts for a large share of Amsterdam's economy; however, the industrial activities that continue are varied, ranging from shipbuilding and heavy engineering to petrochemicals, food processing (including brewing), and diamond polishing. Aimed at reducing unemployment, the city's active economic policy seeks to attract industrial investment by improving infrastructural links with the surrounding region and by providing training, temporary workers, and grants to employers. In the process, the city government created thousands of subsidized jobs toward the end of the 20th century.

Tourism

Tourism of all kinds is a major and growing economic activity. Many visitors to the city come for business purposes or to attend conferences, particularly at the large RAI Exhibition and Congress Centre. Because it is possible to see many of the sites on foot in a single day, day trips to Amsterdam are also extremely popular.

Transportation

Amsterdam commands excellent transport connections via rail, water, road, and air. Schiphol Airport is among the busiest in Europe and indisputably one of the world's major hub airports. Amsterdam's seaport also ranks among the most important in Europe, but, overshadowed by the huge Rotterdam-Europoort nearby, the Amsterdam docks underwent a gradual decline in traffic during the late 20th century. An extensive network of superhighways connects Amsterdam with all parts of the Netherlands and with

Germany and Belgium. Within the city, since the 1960s, planners have favoured public transportation to reduce automobile use. A high-speed metro line opened in 1976, and a new fast rail link to Schiphol entered service in 1988, but trams remain the principal means of transportation in inner Amsterdam, while buses are important in outer districts.

According to the Dutch constitution, every municipality in the Netherlands is headed by a council, whose size depends on the number of inhabitants. The 45 members of the Amsterdam City Council are elected to four-year terms of office. The council's College of Aldermen comprises eight elected aldermen and the mayor, who is appointed by the crown for a period of six years. The mayor also presides at the meetings of the council but is not an official member of this body. Although the council has no say in the appointment of the mayor, the officeholder usually represents the largest political group in the council. Since the end of World War II, the Labour Party has dominated the council, and the mayors have come from its ranks. The council, however, is made up of members of many different political persuasions, including the Greens and the Green Left. Chosen by and from the members of the council, the aldermen are elected to four-year terms. Aldermen also receive an income, while council members are paid only an attendance fee.

As a rule, council meetings are open to the public. From 1655 to 1808 the seat of the council was located on the Dam, where the medieval town hall was replaced by a building designed by the 17th-century Dutch architect Jacob van Campen. When Louis Bonaparte, the French king of Holland, chose this structure as his residence in 1808 and converted it into what is now the Royal Palace (Koninklijk Paleis), the council moved to the Prinsenhof, a onetime convent that later became the Admiralty Court. In the mid-1980s a new city hall and opera house were constructed on the north bank of the Amstel River, at Waterloo Square. In 1926 Herengracht 502, which was built for a director of the Dutch East India Company in 1672, became the mayor's official residence.

The responsibilities of the municipality include public transportation, public works (including acquisition and allocation of grounds and buildings), public health, housing, electricity and gas, the port, markets, police, the fire brigade, sanitation, social services, waterworks, education, and churchyards. The city has its own clearing bank, credit bank, advertising department, printing shop, swimming pools, theatre, archive department, museums, slaughterhouse, and orphanage.

Cultural life

As a centre for the arts, Amsterdam has much to offer. There are some 40 museums, which attract about four million visitors annually. The Rijksmuseum (State Museum) is famous for its collection of 17th-century Dutch masterpieces. The Stedelijk (Municipal) Museum is a leading international collection of modern art. The Van Gogh Museum is dedicated to the work of Vincent van Gogh and his contemporaries. Other important museums include the Anne Frank House, the Amsterdam Historical Museum, the Dutch Maritime Museum, and the Rembrandt House.

There are more than 200 live-performance sites, including the Concertgebouw, which is the home of the world-famous Royal Concertgebouw Orchestra, and the Muziektheater, where the national ballet and opera companies perform. The city is also home to two universities the University of Amsterdam, founded in 1632, and the Free University, founded in 1880 and numerous academies and conservatories. The architecture of the inner city (and of some of the suburbs) is a delight for many tourists interested in culture, who seek out the superbly preserved canal-side mansions of the Golden Age and the numerous historic monuments, including the Royal Palace. The arts play an important economic role in Amsterdam, employing thousands of people and generating nearly $1 billion in revenues annually. There are more than 100 galleries, including major auction houses.

Recreational facilities are extensive. The Amsterdam Woods, the seaside resort of Zandvoort to the west, Sloter Lake (Sloterplas) in the heart of the western suburbs, and many smaller lakes to the south and north of the city all offer opportunities for outdoor recreation. There are about 40 sports parks, clubs for almost every sport, and more than 250 open-air tennis courts in this crowded city. For spectator sports, the Amsterdam Arena, home of the Ajax football (soccer) club, and the Olympic Stadium are world-class venues.

History

Early settlement and growth

Although modern historians do not exclude the possibility that during the Roman period some form of settlement existed at the mouth of the Amstel River, no evidence of one has ever been found. So far as is known, Amsterdam originated as a small fishing village in the 13th century AD. To protect themselves from floods, the early inhabitants had to build dikes on both sides of the river, and about 1270 they built a dam between these dikes.

Even then, merchant ships from Amsterdam sailed as far as the Baltic Sea and laid the foundation of the future trade centre, acting as a link between northern

Europe and Flanders (now northern Belgium and northern France). The city was under the jurisdiction of the counts of Holland, one of whom, Count Floris V, granted the homines manentes apud Amestelledamme ("people living near the Amstel dam") a toll privilege in 1275. This document mentions the name Amsterdam for the first time, though a full charter was not granted until 1306. The city rapidly extended its business, and in 1489, as a sign of gratitude for the support given by the city to the Burgundian-Austrian monarchs, Emperor Maximilian I allowed Amsterdam to adorn its armorial bearings with the imperial crown. By then Holland's greatest commercial town and port, as well as the granary of the northern Netherlands, Amsterdam had become a centre of wealth and influence in Europe.

After the Netherlands passed to the Spanish crown in the 16th century, a religious and political rebellion against Spanish oppression spread across the region. Amsterdam hesitated to join the rebellion led by

William I (the Silent), prince of Orange, but in 1578 there was a bloodless revolution in the city. The magistrates, together with the majority of Roman Catholic priests, were deported; the religious orders and communities were secularized; the Dutch Reformed church effectively replaced the Roman Catholic church; and Amsterdam joined the Dutch rebellion against Spain.

Amsterdam was still a small city with no more than about 30,000 inhabitants, but things changed quickly, especially in 1585, when Spanish troops recaptured Antwerp (in modern Belgium), then the dominant port and commercial centre of the Netherlands. Dutch forces responded by blockading the Schelde River, Antwerp's only access to the sea. The fall of Antwerp led to a wholesale influx of mainly Protestant refugees into the towns of the northern Netherlands, especially Amsterdam. Their arrival enriched the city's intellectual, cultural, and commercial life. Banking and shipbuilding especially flourished. Much of the trade formerly concentrated in Antwerp then moved to Amsterdam, and along with the Flemish merchants soon came hundreds of Jews expelled from Portugal, followed by their coreligionists from the area of modern Germany and eastern Europe. The city soon became a trading metropolis, whose population more than tripled between 1565 and 1618. Merchant ships from Amsterdam not only sailed to the Baltic and the Mediterranean but also plied the long sea route to the East Indies and established colonies in South America and southern Africa.

At this time, the still outwardly medieval town developed into a big city, and in 1612 the city council decided upon a new extension the Three Canals Plan. Furthermore, the city needed a new and stately city hall, and the architect Jacob van Campen was commissioned to build one on Dam square in the shadow of the New Church. In 1632 the Athenaeum Illustre (which became the University of Amsterdam in the 19th century) was erected. When the Treaty of

Münster ended the Eighty Years' War (1568–1648) with Spain, Amsterdam was the financial, trading, and cultural centre of the world, lending money to foreign kings and emperors and thus exerting political influence internationally.

Conflict between the city council and other political forces in the Dutch republic was inevitable because the country was effectively no longer ruled by the States General in The Hague but by a small elite of magistrates and merchants in Amsterdam. This situation led to political difficulties with William II, prince of Orange, who in 1650 planned to besiege the city. Amsterdam, nevertheless, maintained its dominant position for many years. Decline gradually came in the 18th century; London and Hamburg surpassed Amsterdam as trade centres, and London became the financial heart of Europe. Amsterdam was occupied in 1787 by the Prussians, who backed the policy of William V, prince of Orange. The French, welcomed as liberators in 1795, brought freedom, but within a few years trade and shipping nearly stopped because of Napoleon's embargo on trade with Britain. In 1806 Napoleon proclaimed the Netherlands a kingdom, with Amsterdam as its capital, but by 1810 the country was incorporated into the French Empire. Russian Cossacks drove out the French and entered the city in 1813, and, on March 30, 1814, William VI, prince of Orange, was inaugurated as William I, king of the Netherlands, in Amsterdam's New Church.

The modern city

The international trade on which Amsterdam had thrived suffered greatly during the Napoleonic period, and it was only the revival of Dutch rule and commerce in the East Indies in the 1830s that began to restore prosperity to the city. After 1850 sustained growth set in, and the population doubled (to 500,000) by 1900. The East Indian trade and associated manufactures remained the backbone of the economy. The North Sea Canal, built during the 1870s, strengthened the port by providing a direct link to the North Sea. Amsterdam suffered from the disruption of trade during World War I, but modest prosperity resumed in the 1920s. The Great Depression and World War II were especially traumatic for the capital. The German army occupied the Netherlands in 1940, and Allied bombers attacked industrial areas several times. However, the city's severest loss was the deportation of its 70,000 Jewish inhabitants. There were heroic exploits in Amsterdam by the Dutch Resistance and many quiet deeds of valour in protecting those persecuted by the Nazi regime, such as the family of Anne Frank. However, the city's Jews and their old quarter were almost entirely eliminated.

After the war there was a difficult period of reconstruction, but by the 1950s the economy was booming. The Netherlands in the 1950s was not a radical place, and Amsterdam was typically staid and proper. The 1960s, however, brought social and cultural change throughout the Western world, nowhere more so than in Amsterdam, which embraced the libertarian radicalism for which it has been renowned ever since. The reasons for the extraordinary change are still debated but include the long economic boom, the severity of the religious strictures in mainstream Dutch culture in the mid-20th century, and the traditional Dutch tolerance of difference. This radicalism opened the way for the city's relatively open tolerance for recreational drug use and prostitution. During the 1960s and '70s, numerous radical movements arose, some of them highly political and tightly structured, but many of them playful and satirical, based on street theatre. Public demonstrations often turned into confrontations with the increasingly bewildered and beleaguered police. Riots took place at the wedding of Princess (later Queen) Beatrix in 1966 and at her coronation parade in 1980, and demonstrations, confrontations, and riots over a variety of political issues occurred in central Amsterdam repeatedly into the 1980s. During the 1990s the intensity of street protest diminished, but there is still a radicalism in Amsterdam's public life that is hard to find anywhere else.

Travel Guide

Amsterdam combines the unrivaled beauty of the 17th-century Golden Age city center with plenty of museums and art of the highest order, not to mention a remarkably laid-back atmosphere. It all comes together to make this one of the world's most appealing and offbeat metropolises.

Built on a latticework of concentric canals like an aquatic rainbow, Amsterdam is known as the City of Canals but it's no Venice, content to live on moonlight serenades and former glory. Quite the contrary: on nearly every street here you'll find old and new side by side quiet courtyards where time seems to be holding its breath next to contemporary shopping streets like Kalverstraat, and scantily clad women in red-lighted windows by the city's oldest church. Indeed, Amsterdam has as many lovely facets as a 40-carat diamond polished by one of the city's gem cutters. It's certainly a metropolis, but a rather small and very accessible one. Locals tend to refer to it as a big village, albeit one that happens to pack the cultural wallop of a major world destination.

There are scores of concerts every day, numerous museums, summertime festivals, and, of course, a legendary year-round party scene. It's pretty much impossible to resist Amsterdam's charms. With 8,500 registered monuments, many of which began as the residences and warehouses of humble merchants, set on 165 man-made canals, and traversed by 1,700 bridges, Amsterdam has the largest historical inner city in Europe. Its famous circle of waterways, the *grachtengordel,* was a 17th-century urban expansion plan for the rich and is a lasting testament to the city's Golden Age. This town is endearing because of its open, easygoing nature but a reputation for championing sex, drugs, and rock 'n' roll does not alone account for Amsterdam's being one of the most popular destinations in Europe. Consider that within a single square mile the city harbors some of the greatest achievements in Western art, from Rembrandt and Van Gogh to Mondrian. Not to mention that this is one of Europe's great walking cities, with much to discover along the way: tiny alleyways barely visible on the map, curtainless windows offering glimpses of daily life, floating houseboats, hidden *hofjes* (courtyards with almshouses), sudden vistas of church spires, and gabled roofs that look like so many unframed paintings.

Along the way, keep an eye out for joyful detail here and there a bronze breast hidden among cobblestones, or witty stone tablets denoting the trade of a previous owner. And those "XXX" symbols you see all over town are not a mark of the city's triple-X reputation. They're part of Amsterdam's official coat of arms: three St.

Andrew's crosses, believed to represent the three dangers that have traditionally plagued the city flood, fire, and pestilence. The coat's motto ("Valiant, determined, compassionate") was introduced in 1947 by Queen Wilhelmina in remembrance of the 1941 February Strike in Amsterdam, the first time in Europe that non-Jewish people openly protested against the persecution of Jews by the Nazi regime.

Why Go to Amsterdam

Don't believe everything you hear about Amsterdam. Yes, this Netherlands city takes a lax look at women beckoning business in the Red Light District and "coffee shops" selling an unorthodox type of herb to a toking clientele, but these descriptions only scratch the surface. At some point, during an excellent Indonesian meal, a twilight canal-side rambling or a shopping excursion through the boutiques of Nine Little Streets, you'll realize as many travelers have before you that there's much more to Amsterdam than you might've thought.

And although the city's loose laws on vice seem to attract a college-age, male-dominant crowd, Amsterdam is also ideal as a romantic getaway for two or an educational excursion with the kids. With attractions that range from biking along a maze of canals to remembering the Holocaust through the eyes of Anne Frank; from exploring the swirling Expressionism of Vincent van Gogh to lazing in the expansive Vondelpark, Amsterdam suits a variety of traveler tastes

Sightseeing in Amsterdam

ccAmsterdam is not a kind of city that is full of various places of interest, which are well known all over the world. However, the city itself is actually one huge place of interest - its atmosphere, its international spirit, its tolerance and, of course, wonderful channels have made Amsterdam an outstanding city. If you are going to enjoy sightseeing there, we strongly advise all visitors to include boat rides into their travelling program.

What can Amsterdam offer its visitors? In this city travellers can find not only a wide range of historical and cultural places of interest, such as, for example, The Royal Palace or the Rijksmuseum, but also many unique and funny places, such as the Hash-Marijuana-Hemp Museum. In general, Amsterdam is mostly famous for its museums, which keep attracting millions of tourists every year. Probably, it's nearly impossible to find a person, who has never heard of Van Gogh Museum or The House of Anne Frank, and these are not all popular establishments in the city. There are more than 50 different museums in Amsterdam without taking into consideration a great number of wonderful art galleries.

The Royal Palace. The Royal Palace and Dam Square, which is adjacent to it, are situated right in the centre of the city. They have the full right to be called the heart of Amsterdam. The internationally famous

Madame Tussaud's Wax Museum is located nearby. Once The Royal Palace used to be a city hall, and it was not until Napoleon helped his brother Louie to occupy the Dutch throne then it was turned into The Royal Palace. Nowadays, everybody has an opportunity to enter the palace and enjoy the look of its inner premises, and make a walk along its corridors. Of course, all excursions are made only when the palace is not used by the royal family.

Oude Kerk. Many tourists become quite surprised, when they learn that Oude Kerk is situated right in the centre of Red Light District. Surrounded by prostitutes, who offer their services in red-lighted windows, Oude Kerk has somehow managed to save its medieval look. The road near the church is cobbled, and it's quite simple to slip on it when it's raining. The decoration of the church was removed during the Reformation period. There is a legend of the 13th century connected with the church. Once upon a time there lived a man. One day he became very ill and he was very close to death. Since that moment a wafer, which had been given to him during the Eucharist, started appearing in his house.

The man even tried to burn it, but it didn't help. After the death of the man the wafer was kept in one of the chapels. Sometime later the chapel was completely burnt down, but the mysterious wafer survived in that fire again. Since then, many people have made pilgrimage to Oude Kerk in the memory of that miracle. On the 15th of March a special annual ceremonial procession is organized here. The procession traditionally ends near Oude Kerk.

Red Light District. There's simply no sense in visiting Amsterdam without making a walk in notorious Red Light District. Its special atmosphere reigns there not only at night, but also in the daytime. In Red Light District sex for money is openly offered to absolutely everyone. In huge see-through windows decorated with red lights one will see women of all ages and nationalities. However, visitors should not forget about pickpockets, especially on weekends, when Red Light District is crowded with tourists.

Amsterdam Canals. You will see water almost everywhere in Amsterdam, and this fact traditionally amazes visitors. Because of a great number of canals (the exact number of which is 165) some people even call the city "Venice of the North". The main canals of Amsterdam are Singel, Herengracht, Keizergracht, and Prinsengracht. All of them cross the central part of Amsterdam. You will also find numerous firms that organize boat excursions across the canals not far away from the station and Damrak. The only thing that differs them from each other is the length of queues.

Amsterdam Arena. Amsterdam Arena is worth visiting not only if you're a football fan. In summer this place hosts concerts by such well-known bands as Rolling Stones or U2, who are happy to make their performances there. Visitors will be also able to see games with the participation of the famous football club Ajax, of course, if only you are not so unlucky to arrive in Amsterdam during their summer or winter holiday. By the way, real fans of Ajax simply cannot fail to visit a big shop, where they can buy various goods with the logo of their favourite club.

Madame Tussaud's Wax Museum. Madame Tussaud's Wax Museum is located in a fantastic building in the centre of Amsterdam. The museum has four stores; one of them is completely devoted to the history of Amsterdam. This is the place where visitors will be able to see skilfully made wax figures of various European celebrities, sportsmen, culture figures and members of royal families. There is a hall with wax figures of Hollywood stars and another one with figures of well-known persons, such as Gandhi or Einstein. If you want to have a chance to stand really close to your idol, this museum is something you must visit! By the way, don't forget to take a photo camera with you, as you will surely make many funny photos.

The Railway station building. The railway station building of Amsterdam was built in 1889. Initially, it was used as a station for the transportations of goods. The station was projected by a well-known architect Pierre Cuypers, who also planned the building of the Rijksmuseum. The foundation consists of 8 687 wooden posts, because the building is located in a very damp place. The original construction of the building was constantly changed because of a fast growing quantity of transport. Not long ago the front of the station was restored, and today everyone can enjoy its beauty and magnificence.

Family trip to Amsterdam with children

Amsterdam is one of the best destinations among European cities for travelers with kids. Pleasant surprises and interesting entertainment await visitors simply everywhere, starting from the airport. There is a wonderful play zone for children right in the building of Schiphol Airport. The play zone is called Kids' Forest, and it includes several interesting attractions for children of all ages. There is also a special zone for travelers with kids in the airport, where visitors can feed and change clothes of their children.

While speaking about cultural attractions of Amsterdam, it is surely worth noting numerous medieval architectural monuments. Munttoren medieval tower is, definitely, one of the most notable

Artis Royal Zoo remains one of the most frequently visited landmarks of Amsterdam. The zoo is one of the largest and oldest in whole Europe. Founded yet in 1838, today the zoo occupies a large territory and is distinguished by beautiful design. The zoo has become home to more than 700 species of different animals. Travellers will also find numerous exotic plants that were brought to the zoo from different parts of the world. Some open air cages are free to visit, so small guests of the zoo can see animals closer or even touch them. Besides that, there are a marvelous aquarium, terrarium and even an insectarium in Artis Royal Zoo, so a walk in this wonderful place will never be boring.

Older kids will enjoy NEMO Museum. The main purpose of this interesting and unusual place is to show kids and teenagers that science can be very entertaining and fascinating. Visitors of the museum can be witnesses and even participants of numerous interesting tests. In this museum they will learn the basics of chemistry, watch the process of water purification and even learn a lot about one of the newest sciences genetics.

A visit to Kinderkookkafe will become an unforgettable adventure for children, who are keen on culinary. Here they can try on a real chef's hat and robe, and try to cook various interesting dishes under the guidance of a professional chef. The choice of dishes is really wide and young cooks can learn to make sandwiches, pizza, croissants and even home-made cookies.

Efteling Park remains one of the most popular places for walking and rest in fresh air during warm months in Amsterdam. The wonderful park is considered a country level landmark. Founded in 1952, the park was initially named Magic Forest because of fantastic, skillfully made wooden sculptures that depict characters of various famous fairy tales. The park was growing with time and new interesting attractions were added to it. Nowadays, visitors can see cozy gingerbread houses, singing mushrooms and many other interesting play zones that will amaze and entertain children.

Amsterdam Tropical Museum is another wonderful and unusual place perfect for family rest. This museum is located in one of the most beautiful historic buildings of Amsterdam. Here visitors are able to see various entertaining performances, the main idea of which is to help guests learn more about culture and traditions of different nations from all over the world. During such performances visitors of the museum will have an opportunity to get acquainted with magnificent temples and palaces located in remote countries, make a virtual walk on colorful oriental bazaars or charming narrow streets of old cities. Performances of the

Tropical Museum are made primarily for children of all ages and take place there every week.

When it's raining outside, spend a day in TunFun Speelpark that was organized in an old tunnel. This awesome family park features numerous play grounds with spring boards, trampolines and rides. There are special areas with attractions for small children, so kids of all ages will be happy to visit this park. Moreover, TunFun regularly hosts various master classes for kids, and parents are welcome in a cozy café. The park is made in modern urban style that makes it look quite unusual.

Cuisine of Amsterdam for gourmets. Places for dinner best restaurants

Restaurants and coffee houses of Amsterdam usually strike tourists by their diversity. This city will be surely appreciated by admirers of gastronomic tourism. Café Pacifico Restaurant serves the best Mexican cuisine in the city. It is worth noting that there are not many restaurants of this gastronomic direction in Amsterdam. Tacos, meat with spicy sauces, chicken with rice and wonderful desserts - this restaurant is simply perfect for family rest.

Manzano restaurant is located in one of historical buildings of the city. Here you will find home-made cheese of highest quality and widest choice of meat dishes. The restaurant also offers a large choice of fine wine. Ocho restaurant will become the favorite place of rest for lovers of exotic cuisine and grilled food. Roasted chicken with vegetables, pork in honey sauce, salads and exotic drinks - it's just a small part of dishes available in Ocho.

Is Italian cuisine your choice? Then you should certainly the restaurant named Fifteen Amsterdam as the best Italian cuisine in Amsterdam can be tasted in this place. The restaurant also serves Mediterranean specialties. The Pancake Bakery restaurant is the best pastry of the city. The choice of dishes is really wide - you can try more than fifteen types of pancakes standalone. If your aim is to try national cuisine, Moeders Pot should be definitely your choice. This restaurant serves homemade Dutch dishes: farm salad, stamppot and stew. However, this doesn't mean that food connoisseurs have nothing to do here. The choice of gourmet meal is also wide and visitors will be offered to try Moroccan lamb, soup with lobster, other seafood delicacies, and much more. The variety of food options is so wide in Amsterdam that is becomes a problem to make a choice. However, no matter what restaurant you choose, you are most likely to find great service and delicious food.

The opening of Sal Meijer restaurant took place in 1957. This restaurant offers visitors to taste kosher kitchen. Here visitors will find amazingly tasty sandwiches with smoked meat, fish patties, stew with vegetables, homemade sausages and large choice of soups - the restaurant's menu is very diverse. Reasonable prices are another advantage of this place.

Have you ever tried African cuisine? If yes, you will surely want to try a large choice of meat and vegetable dishes, as well as exotic desserts. If no, then simply visit Addis Ababa restaurant and enjoy new gastronomic experiences. African wine and beer will become an excellent addition to dishes. The quality of drinks is really high, so they will be surely appreciated by the admirers of these beverages. The restaurant's interior also deserves the highest praise: national rugs, unusual glassware and paintings depicting African motifs give Addis Ababa its unique charm.

During various gastronomic tours, guests of Amsterdam are welcome to try the most popular national dishes. Of course, travelers can enjoy local food independently by simply visiting the city's restaurants and cafes. Croquettes with various fillings have long become one of the most popular national dishes. Virtually all dining venues offer this delight. It is possible to find croquettes in large supermarkets, small stalls with street food, and in any restaurant specializing in the national cuisine. As a rule, croquettes are cooked from different types of meat and served with a selection of sauces.

Hotel Pulitzer occupies 25 historic houses on a classical Dutch street along a canal. These buildings were constructed in the 17th 18th centuries, and after restoration they were merged

Sáte is a no less meat dish. This dish looks like small meat skewers with vegetables. It is believed that this dish became popular in the period when the Netherlands had a large colony in Indonesia. The national cuisine of the latter contains many skewers with beef, pork, or chicken. However, skewers in Indonesia are traditionally served with the peanut sauce.

Bami Goreng is one more dish that is present in the vast majority of Amsterdam restaurants specializing in the national cuisine. This dish is made of noodles cooked with various meat and vegetables in a wok.

Numerous restaurants offer this dish in accordance with various signature recipes. Chicken, beans, and soy sprouts remain the most frequently used ingredients offered with noodles. This delicious dish also has Indonesian roots, so all fans of oriental cuisine will be simply in love with it.

Hotel De L Europe Amsterdam is located in a heritage building that belongs to the Victorian period. The story of this site started yet in 1492, when a fortress was built there. Approximately

Sweet tooth travelers also will not be disappointed with their stay in Amsterdam. They will genuinely enjoy Oliebollen dessert that is traditionally served in winter. Small Oliebollen donuts have been cooked in accordance with the unchanged recipe starting from the 17th century. The round shaped donuts are cooked in quite an interesting way local chefs now use special ice cream spoons to make the ideal shape. Raisins are an essential part of the dough. Sometimes, these donuts have apple filling. They are traditionally served with sugar powder. The recipe is considered a "winter" one because Oliebollen are traditionally available before Christmas. However, tourists can also try Oliebollen during various national holidays, at fair trades and festivals.

Amsterdam's traditional national dishes are simple, hearty, and affordable. Boerenkool Stamppot is a great example of that. It is traditional mash with cabbage that is usually offered with meat or sausages. Absolutely every national cuisine restaurant has a selection of affordable dishes, and Boerenkool Stamppot is one of them. It is also often sold in street food stalls and supermarkets.

Traditions & lifestyle

Colors of Amsterdam - traditions, festivals, mentality and lifestyle

Residents of Amsterdam have always been famous for honesty and sincerity, as well as thrift (this concerns many issues, for example, respect to environment). A rich man here will never show his high position and try to attract attention. Moderation in everything this is one of the main traits of this nation's character. The locals are very friendly; they greet everyone, even in public transport and stores. This fact often surprises visitors.

When dealing with the natives, do not express the feeling of superiority as it will certainly cause a lot of negative emotions. Loyalty to distribution and use of soft drugs and has also long become a hallmark of the local way of life. It is worth noting attraction and respect for everything made in the UK from the side of the local residents. Many people here speak English perfectly and are well aware of the lifestyle, culture and worldview of the British.

As it has been mentioned already, the locals show much respect and care for the environment, so visitors of the city will also need to show respect and in no way disturb the natural harmony of this place. The local people are very hospitable and are always ready to help. Probably, this is one of the reasons why

Amsterdam remains a popular tourist destination for so many years. Tulip remains one of the most famous symbols of the Netherlands. Each April the grand opening of Keukenhof Park is held in Amsterdam. This is one of most beloved and anticipated national holidays of the country. Every year several millions of tulip bulbs are planted in this beautiful park, so in spring Keukenhof is painted in all colors of a rainbow. The period starting from April and up to May is the time for colorful fair trades dedicated to flowers. Late summer is the time for a large sale of tulip bulbs, which attracts florists from all countries of the world.

Another striking feature of Amsterdam is the abundance of road cyclists. Many citizens choose two-wheel transportation because of their beliefs. This way they show their care for the environment. Many people use bicycles simply to prevent themselves from spending hours in traffic jams. You will certainly see a big bicycle parking near each public institution. By the way, sometimes it's really hard to find a free space in such parking lot.

Amsterdam is a unique and famous world capital for its legal prostitution and use of soft drugs, gay pride, food festivals and even euthanasia. This becomes even more important to the fashion industry, traditions, art, various festivals, carnivals, and festivities. When talking about Amsterdam, the first association coming to one's mind is a notorious Red Light District and weed coffee shops. The so-called Cannabis Cup is a famous annual festival, which happens at the end of autumn. Tourists and visitors can enjoy the competition between small coffee shops, which serve munchies with a "secret" ingredient. Such competitions have a special panel of judges and only for €200, you can become its member!

Everything you have heard about the Red Light District is the truth: prostitutes in the red-light windows, vice houses, haze-filled bars and cafes, sex-shops and strip-shows. When strolling around the neighborhood - be careful and watch out for pocket lifters. Also be aware of that it's forbidden to take photos and videos of the prostitutes in the windows this will be taken as the sign of the disrespect, and you can say "good-bye" to your camera as well. Here you can legally purchase up to 5 grams of marijuana, space cakes, hashish, and truffles. This amount is legal, tolerated and will not be prosecuted by the authorities.

Already old hat that lots carnivals take place at every step, so each and one tourist will find an activity after his or her own heart. In April tourists have a brilliant opportunity to witness annual Flower Parade or Bloemencorso in Dutch. The procession consists of 20 huge floats and 30 decorated carts that carry and display the flower masterpieces. But you need to come early to find a good spot and enjoy the procession. Thousands of native people and visitors abroad gather at Noordwijk, from where all the floats pass a long way (42 km) to Haarlem. In Haarlem, next day, you can admire all the flower installations where the floats remain till the evening.

Amsterdam is well-known for its open mind towards equality of the gay, lesbian and transgender communities. In the middle of summer, you have a chance to observe the Amsterdam Gay Pride one of the world's largest celebrations that last for a week. During this week you can party, visit galleries and art exhibitions, cinema and sports events hosted by gay communities and be welcomed. In love with dance and music festivals? In summer you can enjoy your time at Pitch or Verknipt Festival, Buiten Westen or Dekmantel Weekender. Traveling with family? Take them to Sail Amsterdam and watch the most impressive sailing ships in Amsterdam Harbor, or Artis ZOOmeravonden and learn about various nocturnal rituals animals have.

Culture: sights to visit

Culture of Amsterdam. Places to visit - old town, temples, theaters, museums and palaces

Amsterdammers officially speak Dutch, but most residents also speak English and it's insulting to think otherwise. If you're versed, try to speak a little Dutch:

hallo for "hello" and *dank u* for "thank you." But don't patronize Amsterdammers by asking, "Do you speak English?"

"Going Dutch" is more a way of life than an expression. The Dutch are notorious for their frugality yet they also have a large appetite for consumerism, so you can enjoy "going Dutch" by shopping. Amsterdam's official currency is the euro (EUR). Since the euro to U.S. dollar exchange rate fluctuates often, be sure to check what the current exchange rate is before you go. Major credit cards are accepted at most restaurants and shops.

Marijuana use in Amsterdam is tolerated though not legal. As of 2016, Amsterdam has implemented the following rules for its coffee shops: no one younger than 18 can be admitted, no alcohol can be served, shops cannot be located within 350 meters of a school and consumption is limited to .5 grams a day

While speaking about cultural attractions of Amsterdam, it is surely worth noting numerous medieval architectural monuments. Munttoren medieval tower is, definitely, one of the most notable sights of this place. The building of the tower was completed in the end of the 15th century. The tower was reconstructed in the 17th century and so today guests can visit this magnificent architectural monument of the Renaissance. Montelbaanstoren Tower is a no less interesting attraction. This tower was built in the beginning of the 16th century. The tower served as a protective facility during the Middle Ages. Nowadays it is used as the main office of the city's water management.

Jewish Historical Museum (Joods Historisch Museu) is a noteworthy place among the cultural institutions of the city. The museum is located in an old synagogue. Its opening took place in 1987. Many artifacts have been lost during the war, but even this modern collection of artifacts looks very impressive. Pathé Tuschinski

Theatre was opened in 1921. Today this theater is considered one of most striking sights of the city. A unique combination of architectural styles and an unforgettable design of the facade and lobby make all visitors stop in admiration for nearly a century. The full reconstruction of the building was completed in 2002. Nowadays a cinema is opened in it.

Dam Square is the location of the famous historical monument - National Monument (Nationaal Monument). It was opened in 1956 in the memory of victims of World War II. Every year on May 4 a solemn wreath-laying ceremony takes place at the memorial. You will find much pleasure simply in making a usual walk through the city's streets as you will find many interesting museums and galleries there. Some of the local cultural institutions are truly unusual, for example, Museum of Hashish and Marijuana. This is the only institution of this kind in the world. Museum of Tattoos was opened in 1995. It has also quickly gained popularity among holidaymakers. During the excursion visitors will see numerous interesting decorations and ornaments from ancient times till the present. The museum has an interesting thematic literature. It is visited by more than twenty thousand people each year.

In addition to the aforementioned Museum of Hashish and Marijuana, the city has a Cannabis College (located very close by), where you can look at cannabis and marijuana bushes, as well as learn a lot of new and interesting information about what can be made from the plants. And, of course, Amsterdam cannot be imagined without visiting the popular coffee shop called Dampkring. It is famous for the fact that it was here that some episodes of the film "Ocean's twelve" were shot. The institution is very much loved by movie fans due to its ambience, and places here are always occupied.

Another unique museum in the city is the Sexmuseum Venustempel. Where else can it be located, if not in a city of tolerance and avant-garde? Among its exhibits, there are erotic retrography, a sculpture of Marilyn Monroe depicting a scene from the extremely popular film "The Seven Year Itch", as well as wax moving figures. By the way, the famous Madame Tussaud's Wax Museum is also situated in the capital of the Netherlands. Here you can look at the figures of Angela Merkel, Jennifer Lopez, Johnny Depp, Adele, Princess Diana and even characters from the comic book Marvel, among them Thor and the Iron Man. Another interesting museum is Body Worlds, which will be interesting to visit even with children. Here you can learn a lot of new things about the human anatomy but it is much more interesting how this information is presented.

However, Amsterdam is not only all about museums dedicated to "the forbidden fruit". When it comes to architectural aesthetics, the city has beautiful buildings. It would be imprudent not to go see them. Among them, Huis met de Hoofden and Huis met de Kabouters. The houses are remarkable in the beauty of their façade. For Amsterdam they are very unusual, which is why the locals enjoy looking at them. Another institution where you can acquire knowledge is the scientific center Nemo. The museum is unique in that you are allowed to touch the exhibits here, and you can bring all the "inquisitive kids" with you their questions will be answered here immediately.

The Netherlands is famous for its mills (this is one of the symbols of the country). It is therefore impossible to imagine a traditional tour of the capital of the country of tulips without visiting the amazing mills De Gooyer and De Riekermolen, just as it is impossible to imagine a tour of Amsterdam without visiting the "Eiffel Tower" of the city. Function is served by A'DAM Lookout a place that you can climb onto to "hang out" for a long time, admiring the panorama of the city and at that time it "opens its soul". Also worthy of note is Royal Coster Diamonds. It is considered a historic site, because it was here that the legendary Kohinoor was cut (it is now stored in the Tower as part of the treasures of the Crown of Great Britain).

Attractions & nightlife

City break in Amsterdam. Active leisure ideas for Amsterdam - attractions, recreation and nightlife
Cycling around the city remains one of the main entertainments, which is very popular among tourists. Virtually every part of the city has a special bicycle area, so you can easily rent this unpretentious vehicle and go exploring the local sights. MacBike Bicycle Rental, Frederic Bike, Het Zwarte Fietsenplan and Damstraat Offer are known as best bike rental centers.

Fans of beach rest will surprisingly find entertainment here. The best beaches of Amsterdam are Zandvoort and Ijmuiden. The night life of the city is worth a separated article. On the territory of the city you will find a large number of clubs, night bars, discos and coffee shops. The majority of venues working at night can be found in Red Light District near Rembrandtplein District and Leidseplein Square.

Paradiso Club, which is located near the city's center, is very popular among both tourists and residents. In this club you will find music of different styles. Besides excellent musical accompaniment this club attracts visitors by its richest choice of drinks. Melkweg Club never ceases to delight visitors by its interesting entertainment programs. Here you will be able to attend theme parties, vivid theatrical plays, and performances by musical groups, as well as various presentations. Sugar Factory Club is a place with a really mysterious atmosphere. The club has become a permanent place for performances of popular musicians and theater groups.

Those visitors, who enjoy noisy parties and cannot imagine a holiday without energetic dances, will surely like Exit Night Club. Here is played music of different fields, and parties are often accompanied by costumed shows and interesting performances. The interior of Jimmy Woo Club is made in the unique oriental style. The dance floor of the club resembles a classic Hong

Kong disco. It is worth noting that this club has a strict dress code, so you should definitely pay some attention on your look before you go to it.

Shopping fans should definitely visit the market, which is located on Waterlooplein Square. Here you can buy memorable souvenirs, handmade crafts, and antiques. If you enjoy drinking coffee, we suggest attending Bulldog chain of cafes dedicated to this amazing drink. These are special facilities for tourists. Other popular coffee shops are The Bluebird and Grey Area.

Amsterdam offers its visitors a broad range of recreational activities: indoor karting and skiing, race-car driving and kite-surfing, snowboarding and climbing. At the Snow Planet an amazing indoor slope you can enjoy skiing and snowboarding, but dress good the temperature is quite low here. The prices per various kind of activities start from €16. Always wanted to try driving the kart or racing car? Then you should go straight to the Race Planet. It is a huge all-weather leisure center, where you will find bowling area, the arena for laser games, and two karting tracks.

Skateboarding fans have a chance to participate in the Friday Night Skate. This skating weekend takes place each Friday during the year. Skaters gather at Vandelpark, where they roll twenty kilometers through Amsterdam. Have fun at the Climbing wall near the Amsterdam Central Station, the activity for those who are not scared of height. Love water activities? Then go straight to the Wind Water Beach, which is located near Amsterdam's River IJ. Here you will have the greatest time here, while sky-surfing and sailing. At the Port of Amsterdam, you can sunbathe, admire marvelous panorama and fill your tummy with top-notch food and drinks.

Have you seen Amsterdam from the bird's eye view? No, but you desire so? Then skydiving is the best option for you. Amsterdam parachuting services can be found on the outskirts of the city. In Amsterdam, you will find a sky-diving club near to the international airport. A brilliant view of Rotterdam, North Sea, and a marvelous panoramic view is guaranteed. Amsterdam is the city of contrasts, with its vice quarters and cultural landmarks, deep cultural roots, and open-minded people.

Tips for tourists

Preparing your trip to Amsterdam: advices & hints - things to do and to obey

1. Smoking in public places is prohibited in Amsterdam. You will have to forget even about usual nicotine cigarettes to meet this social rule.

2. Visitors are advised not to overeat cakes with cannabis and mushrooms, which can be acquired in smart shops. No more than three pancakes per day are considered safe.

3. We do not recommend buying SuperShiva in coffee shops. It has very depressing impact on the unprepared tourists.

4. Weather in Amsterdam is very unpredictable, so all residents always carry a raincoat with them. Travelers will also make a right decision if they get some protection from the rain. Those, who enjoy walking, will feel fine if they take an umbrella with them, and a raincoat is more suitable in case you ride a bicycle.

5. Those tourists, who plan to travel around the city, use public transport, and visit cultural institutions, are recommended to buy a special tourist pass in VVV service. It gives the right to use public transport for free and provides tourists with discounts when visiting museums.

6. Fans of flowers should visit a flower market located in the heart of the city. Only here you can buy a huge bouquet made of 50 fragrant tulips for just 5 Euro.

7. Fans of shopping are recommended to visit shops and trading centers in the morning. In the afternoon and on weekends all shopping streets of the city are crowded with numerous people, so looking at shop windows will be rather problematic.

8. A walk to the local antique store can replace a trip to a museum. Kind sellers will offer guests fresh coffee and will entertain them with interesting stories, but to thank for the entertainment a buyer will be simply required to purchase a souvenir.

9. It may be quite difficult to travel on the streets of Old Town on a bicycle. There are no special bike lanes here, so there are often traffic jams on all main routes.

What to visit being in Amsterdam - unique sights

Hash Marihuana Hemp Museum
Some museum rooms are dedicated to breeding the exhibits - here the various hemp varieties cultivated by the museum staff grow. Since 2003, the large and constantly updated collection of exhibits has been located in the new building, not far from Dam Square. Today, the museum's guests can see more than 6,000

unique exhibits. Although the theme of the museum is quite contradictory and controversial, the numerous tourists have been receiving it for several years. It must be borne in mind that the children under 13 years of age can visit the museum of marijuana free of charge, but only accompanied by adults

Year: 1991.

The guests of Amsterdam have a unique opportunity to visit the Museum of Marijuana. Such a facility can hardly be imagined in any other city in the world. The museum was opened in 1991. Its founder was Ben Dronkers, for whom the breeding of hemp became the life-work. Visitors to the museum will learn that hemp is one of the oldest grasses on the planet, which has long been applied.

The hemp was used for cooking, from this grass the remedies were made of many diseases and even fabric and paper. The large collection of exhibits illustrates this remarkable fact: in the museum one can see the old medical books and recipes, the beautiful clothes and even the old Heupräparate. Part of the exposure is dedicated to 'the smoke side of the question'. Here is a rich collection of old pipes, shisha and other smoking accessories presented.

Some museum rooms are dedicated to breeding the exhibits - here the various hemp varieties cultivated by the museum staff grow. Since 2003, the large and constantly updated collection of exhibits has been located in the new building, not far from Dam Square. Today, the museum's guests can see more than 6,000 unique exhibits. Although the theme of the museum is quite contradictory and controversial, the numerous tourists have been receiving it for several years. It must be borne in mind that the children under 13 years of age can visit the museum of marijuana free of charge, but only accompanied by adults.

Sauna Deco

In the 1970s, the department store, which was known for its exquisite interior design, was renovated. After the renovation, most decor elements were abolished.

These magnificent decor elements of the historical department store were brought into the sauna of Amsterdam. Today its visitors can go to the pool on a unique wooden staircase, over which several decades ago Parisians went shopping. Tourists who decide to visit the most famous and popular sauna in the Netherlands, should observe an important rule - wearing a bathing suit in sauna is strictly prohibited

A real landmark of national importance for the Netherlands is a Deco sauna, located in Amsterdam. This small sauna, located in the heart of the city, is a true embodiment of the Art Deco style. In its interior there is a variety of exquisite elements made of bronze. A special charm of the room is attached to stained glass windows and unique antiques.

A real Turkish hammam is available to visitors of the Deco complex, as well as two saunas and a hydromassage pool. A courtyard is equipped with a beautiful seating area with a terrace and a garden. Another attractive feature of the sauna is a high-class massage parlor, which employs some of the best specialists in the city. The history of the bath complex is very interesting and inextricably linked to the famous Parisian department store Le Bon Marche.

In the 1970s, the department store, which was known for its exquisite interior design, was renovated. After the renovation, most decor elements were abolished. These magnificent decor elements of the historical department store were brought into the sauna of Amsterdam. Today its visitors can go to the pool on a unique wooden staircase, over which several decades ago Parisians went shopping. Tourists who decide to visit the most famous and popular sauna in the Netherlands, should observe an important rule - wearing a bathing suit in sauna is strictly prohibited

Unusual weekend

How to spend top weekend in Amsterdam - ideas on extraordinary attractions and sites

Always crowded and popular with tourists, Amsterdam has many interesting and unusual places. One of them can be found in Hortus Botanicus. This botanic garden was established yet in the first part of the 17th century and is known as one of the most famous and beautiful gardens in whole Europe. It is so big that not all visitors have enough stamina to see all interesting places of the garden during an excursion. When visiting it, don't forget to attend the magnificent "subtropical greenhouse". There is a fancy bridge in the greenhouse, from which visitors will enjoy an adorable view of ferns and blooming trees.

Travellers, who are interested not only in sightseeing, but also in tasting local cuisine, should not limit themselves to eating in restaurants only. Pannenkoeken have become one of gastronomic symbols of the Netherlands. These delicious pancakes are served with different fillings and are distinguished not only by an original way of cooking, but also by quite an unusual way of serving. Experienced foodies know that the best place to taste this national dish is to visit The Pancake Bakery hat is located not far away from the Anne Frank Museum. Here visitors can choose from 70 different types of the popular national dish. The bakery will also please with its affordable prices.

Red Light District has been known as one of the most famous symbols of Amsterdam. Besides sex shops and various entertaining venues, the area has some interesting landmarks. One of the most extravagant monuments in the city is also located here. This is a bronze relief depicting a hand caressing a female breast. The monument is installed right in the ground and that makes it even more unusual. There are many legends connected with that monument. It is believed that it is particularly beneficial for men as those men who touch it are guaranteed to have male power and rich sexual life.

Those, who are tired of visiting classical museums, are recommended to head to Amsterdam Tattoo Museum This museum was founded by Henk Schiffmacher, famous tattoo master. The opening of the museum took place in Amsterdam in 2011. Currently, the venue exhibits more than 40,000 items that are somehow connected to tattoo making. Having observed the museum and its exhibition, do not hurry to leave the area. There is an interesting book store near it, where it is possible to buy various books dedicated to tattoos. If you like modern art, then wait till Sunday and head to Spui Plein On weekends, the square turns into a large and very popular art market. This is the place where travelers can see works of the most famous and talented artists of Amsterdam. It is possible not only to observe, but also to purchase the works that you like. Besides art, people come to the market to listen to live music as this is one of rare places where it is possible to see street musicians play on harps.

There are many parks in Amsterdam, and each of them has its own interesting peculiarities and places of interest. If the idea of seeing one of the most symbolic and unusual park monuments sounds appealing, head to Leidseplein Square and find the Hotel American that is located close to it. Then move south-west and you will reach a small charming park that is not known to the majority of travelers. In the park, find the old sycamore tree and look at its branches. There is a tiny figure of a human with a saw. This monument is a vivid illustration of the famous proverb "don't cut the bough you are standing on". The author of the statue and the time when it was installed are not clearly known. According to a theory, the monument was made by a local and it appeared in the park in the 80s of the previous century.

Where to stay?

Extraordinary hotels

Best choice for your unusual city break in Amsterdam

The development of design hotel Hotel Droog was made by Renny Ramakers, head of famous boutique shop and show room. The hotel is located in the centre of Amsterdam close to Waterloo Square. This is a very unusual hotel that looks nothing like ordinary hotels we all know. Its design was developed by Droog studio that specializes on avant-garde projects. The area of 700 sq. metres has become home to several shops, exhibitions and a beauty salon, all of which can be freely visited by guests of the hotel. Travellers are also welcome to rest in a wonderful garden that was created by French designers Claude Pasquer and Corinne Dtroyat.

Hotel Filosof is a thematic hotel in the central district of Amsterdam. Conveniently located on a calm street not far away from Vondelpark, the hotel occupies several buildings constructed in the 19th century. It has only 38 guestrooms, each of which is dedicated to one great philosopher Aristotle, Spinoza, Nietzsche, Karl Marx, Confucius and others. All the guestrooms are furnished with awesome elegance and reflex the main idea of the hotel. There are books and busts of famous scientists on shelves, and walls are decorated with paintings and quotes of great philosophers.

The next hotel that is worth mentioning is Qbic Hotel WTC , which was recently open in the building of World Trading Centre. Guestrooms of this hotel were developed and furnished by Dutch designers, who were inspired by the idea of a capsule hotel. In such a hotel, not much is needed for convenient rest. All guestrooms come with comfortable beds, a work desk and a shower. Every guestroom has a stylish lightning system that adds futurism to the design and makes guestrooms look like a spacecraft's cabin. This hotel attracts travellers with its relatively low prices together with high level of comfort. There is no better proof of popularity than occupancy, and guestrooms at this hotel need to be booked in advance as during its first year of work the occupancy reached 99%.

One more unique hotel can be found in the northern part of the IJ Bay. This is Faralda Crane that is located on the territory of a former dock yard. The hotel is located in quite an original place an old dockside crane that previously belonged to NDSM Company.

Nowadays, the rebuilt crane has become home to a local TV studio and a unique hotel with only three luxurious guestrooms made in fantasy style. Guests of the hotel can select guestrooms located at the height of 35, 40 or 45 metres. All the guestrooms feature magnificent panoramic views of the area. The hotel has become very popular with couples. The roof of the crane was rebuilt into a spacious terrace with Jacuzzi. Such an original hotel will also be liked by fans of bungee jumping.

Travellers, who prefer to stay in unusual places, will simply fall in love with Hotel de Windketel. This hotel is located in an old water tower that was saved only thanks to efforts of local people. The hotel is located not far away from an old gas factory. Currently, this factory is a part of Westergasfabriek. The small octagonal water tower was built yet in 1897. With time, the tower was not used for its original purpose anymore and was on the verge of destruction. Several local people, who lived in neighbor houses, decided to save the historic building and open an original designer made guestroom in the tower. The guestroom has everything needed for comfortable long-term stay in Amsterdam a cozy bedroom, well-equipped kitchen and living room, and the ground level of the water tower was turned into a dining room.

Stylish Design Hotels

Collection of top unique boutique hotels

Amsterdam suburbs, on the bank of the Amstel River, have become the location of a very interesting place. This attractive area with fresh air and nature of the countryside was once home for workers' barracks that were built in yet in the 18th century. The barracks steadily lost their importance, but they didn't turn into dust thanks to efforts of two people Dutch designer Marcel Wanders and restaurateur Pieter Lute. Together they created a true miracle, a hotel that attracts visitors from all corners of Europe. Seven old barracks were turned into a designer boutique hotel Lute Suites. All the houses are made in ultra-modern style and every guestroom at this hotel is a true piece of art. Marcel Wanders decided to decorate walls with mosaics and baroque panels. He added interior elements designed by himself, such as soap dish shaped bathtubs, knitted armchairs, plastic lamps, but at the same time he preserved historic items and original elements of design.

Stylish and fashionable, WestCord Fashion is located opposite International Fashion Centre. The idea of haute couture was the biggest inspiration for designers of the hotel. Halls, restaurant and bar of the hotel feature mannequins dressed in fancy outfits. Walls are decorated with advertising posters, paintings and glass racks with women accessories. Visitors of the hotel will feel like they have entered a temple of couture. Spacious guestrooms of the hotel are no less stylish and comfortable.

Andaz Amsterdam Prinsengracht belongs to the Andaz brand. One can find these hotels in different countries of the world. However, this hotel is distinguished by its own unique style as its owners had an idea of changing traditional standards of the hospitality industry and creating something new and original. Inner premises were designed by Marcel Wanders who is famous for his unusual projects. The atmosphere of this hotel is the reflection of the Dutch capital and its culture and historic heritage. The biggest collection of video installations in the world only adds charm to this fascinating place. Halls and guestrooms of the hotel feature works of artists from all over the world. Many zones in the hotel have items developed and designed by Wanders himself, so visitors will have a wonderful opportunity to enjoy the work of the famous master.

The area of Zaandam, which is located in Amsterdam suburbs, is home to an interesting hotel with very unusual design - Inntel Hotel Amsterdam Zaandam . The outer design of the hotel slightly resembles a pyramid of traditional colored small Dutch houses that make the hotel very eye-catching. The building consists of seventy 12-story houses. The building looks like a skyscraper that rises above the suburban area and looks very fancy from all angles. All guestrooms are made to provide guests with pleasant and trouble-free relaxation, exactly how it was intended by the design team who tried to create "a home away from home". Walls of guestrooms are decorated with detailed photographs of cheese, delicious biscuits and cookies. Such unusual photos might have been added because Zaandam is famous for its god-like biscuits that are well-known far beyond the borders of the town.

art'otel Amsterdam is located right in the heart of the city not far away from the railway station. This hotel will surely amaze fans of modern art. The design of the hotel was developed by best professionals of designer studio Atelier Van Lieshout. Simply every detail in this hotel is original and unusual. Guests will find in this hotel luxurious designer furniture with unusual shapes, unique paintings and sculptures made of polished metal, walls and ceilings decorated with skillful artworks. The hotel is located in the same building with multifunctional entertainment centre 5&33 that includes a fine restaurant and a bar, a stylish lounge and a library, and even a public library that regularly hosts different interesting events.

Luxury Accommodation

Top places to stay in Amsterdam - most luxury and fashionable hotels

Luxurious and modern Dylan Hotel is located in a restored building of a former theatre. The hotel includes 33 standard guestrooms and 8 suites. As the guestrooms are located on top of the building, the large windows offer panoramic views of the city centre and its beautiful canals. Every guestroom has a name, its own unique color and theme. The designer used oriental style, Chinese and Japanese furniture throughout the hotel. This ideal hotel has simply everything needed for a leisure or business traveller quality service, convenient location in the heart of historic centre and healthy food.

Okura Hotel is a luxurious hotel that is always present in the rating of Amsterdam hotels. Elegantly designed guestrooms come with up-to-date equipment lightning control stations, LCD TV and other gadgets on night tables on every side of the bed. Bathrooms are decorated with marble and come with modern bathtubs. To the service of guests there are four restaurants; one of them, a French cuisine restaurant, is awarded with two Michelin stars and a Japanese restaurant is considered the best in the city. Guests of this posh hotel can also attend the best wellness club in the city - Executive Health Club.

Grand Amrâth Amsterdam is a five star hotel that occupies the building of a former shipping company. This monumental building is located near the canal, so its windows offer absolutely stunning views of the city. Beautifully decorated guestrooms feature a wonderful mix of past and modern. Every visitor will value comfort of this magnificent hotel large convenient beds, cozy feather down blankets, a free mini-bar and

Nespresso coffee maker only add to overall satisfaction of hotel guests. There is a free spa centre at the hotel, where guests can enjoy sauna, hydro massage pool or simply relax in a peaceful lounge zone. The Seven Seas restaurant offers international cuisine dishes.

The most prestigious hotel in Amsterdam, Intercontinental Amstel, is located right on the bank of the Amstel River not far away from the legendary theatre of Carre. The large eye-catching building of the hotel has become a true landmark of the city. The grandiose hotel belongs to the largest hotel chain in the world, which guarantees high quality service. Large and luxurious guestrooms of the hotel are mostly designed in red and blue patterns. This hotel makes impression of an old posh European mansion, where every guest will feel privileged. Stylish Victorian décor in this hotel is perfectly combined with all amenities and services that are craved by modern travelers. The hotel's Michelin awarded restaurant serves dishes of the Mediterranean cuisine. Travellers are also welcome in a wellness club with an in-door swimming pool and several massage rooms.

Make a several minute long walk from Dam Square, and you will reach luxurious Crowne Plaza Amsterdam City Centre , which is considered one of the best hotels in Amsterdam. Travellers will find here posh club style guestrooms with king size beds. All guestrooms feature modern technologies and Nespresso coffee makers. Besides elegant guestrooms, there is a magnificent restaurant at the hotel, where guests are welcome to try popular international cuisine dishes as well as typical Dutch dishes.

Even most discerning travelers will be pleased with their stay at NH Collection Krasnapolsky that is open in a beautiful building of the 19th century. The hotel features over 460 guestrooms designed in different color schemes and styles. Many guestrooms have walls decorated with designer wallpapers depicting city life and upscale modern furniture. The majority of suites have large floor-to-ceiling panoramic windows and some guestrooms come with own fully furnished terrace or a large balcony. Every morning breakfast is served in the picturesque interior garden, and the hotel's cozy café is a great place to try exclusive dishes and desserts.

Historical Hotels

Preserved history of Amsterdam: long-standing and historical hotels

Hotel Pulitzer

Hotel Pulitzer occupies 25 historic houses on a classical Dutch street along a canal. These buildings were constructed in the 17th 18th centuries, and after restoration they were merged into one hotel. Luckily, the houses are still furnished with old classical Dutch items, but that doesn't mean the hotel is inconvenient as together with its antique design it offers all modern services and amenities. The hotel has 230 guestrooms, each of which has its own style and represents a part of Dutch history and culture. Having kept the original heavy wooden beams, designers succeeded in retaining historic atmosphere of this place. The hotel has an adjusting garden, inside which guests will find an open picture gallery. A private quay with boats is another advantage of this hotel as guests can use the boats and make an excursion ride on canals.

NH Barbizon Palace

The historic centre of Amsterdam has become home to NH Barbizon Palace that occupies 19 houses, the majority of which were built in the 17th century. After a full restoration it has become one of the most famous hotels in the city. This luxurious complex is connected to a 15th century chapel by a system of underground passages. Nowadays, the chapel is used as event space and includes 11 conference halls. The design of the hotel's lobby is simply magnificent marble columns, balconies, a posh staircase and oak wooden beams emphasize traditional Dutch style. Elegant modern furniture only adds luxury to this grandiose hotel. Travellers are recommended not to forget to visit the famous Vermeer restaurant, in which dishes are served in historic atmosphere of the 17th century.

Seven Bridges Hotel is surrounded by the most beautiful canals and historic buildings of the city. The hotel is open in a historic building constructed more than 300 years ago. The hotel has only 11 guestrooms of luxury level. Owners of the hotel decided to keep the antique furniture left from people, who lived in the house centuries ago. Old buffets, hand-made and carved tables and beds, oriental carpets and fine antique items in baroque style make this hotel stand out from the list of exclusive hotels in Amsterdam. Naturally, such individuality and atmosphere of antiquity attract many travelers from all over the world. Breakfasts at this hotel are served in fine china directly in guestrooms.

The area near DeLaMar theatre is the location of a truly unique hotel - Hampshire Hotel - Amsterdam American. The opening of this historic hotel took place yet in 1900. Its design is an amazing combination of art deco and modern designer elements. The historic building of the hotel still has the original design in some of its premises. Besides antique furniture, there are a large collection of old black-and-white photographs, paintings of famous European artists and other antiquities that remind of the culture of the beginning of the 20th century.

Dikker en Thijs Fenice Hotel

The central part of the city is the location of another prestigious hotel, Dikker en Thijs Fenice Hotel This hotel is open in one of the most beautiful historic buildings of Amsterdam. Constructed yet in the 18th century, many years ago the building of the hotel was used as a warehouse of De Prins Company. All guestrooms of the hotel are designed in accordance with traditions of the past, and some guestrooms still have the original wooden beams. Inside the rooms, guests will find massive wooden furniture and elegant tapestries.

Park Plaza Victoria Amsterdam

Park Plaza Victoria Amsterdam is located right opposite the central railway station. This hotel is designed in the style of the 50s of the previous century. Travellers will find here spacious rooms with high ceilings, walls decorated with vintage wallpapers and interesting paintings in massive wooden frames. All guestrooms feature original wooden furniture. Public zones are no less beautiful and deserve separate attention. The hotel is located in a historic building, so its public zones are truly fascinating with their high rise columns, archways and wooden decor elements.

Romantic Hotels

Amsterdam legends. Famous hotels glorified by history or celebrities

Hotel De L Europe Amsterdam

Hotel De L Europe Amsterdam is located in a heritage building that belongs to the Victorian period. The story of this site started yet in 1492, when a fortress was built there. Approximately 140 years later the fortress was demolished and a tavern with guest house were built instead. Only 200 years later famous architect Willem Hamer rebuilt this building made of rock stones and red bricks, completing the design that has survived till our days. The hotel is often called "the second royal palace of Amsterdam". It belongs to the richest family of the Netherlands Heineken and is considered the most luxurious hotel in the city. Just like in a museum, halls of the hotel are decorated with paintings of Dutch artists. These paintings belong to the personal collection of Alfred Heineken. The new wing of the hotel, Dutch Masters Wing, exhibits exact copies of masterpieces that can be seen in the Rijksmuseum. Travellers, who want something special, can book the luxurious Signature Suite with six bedrooms. The legendary hotel has always been a choice of the wealthy and celebrities from all over the world.

Hilton Amsterdam

Hilton Amsterdam is a great choice for business travelers. This hotel is located near a canal and has its own quay, a spacious open terrace and a charming roofed terrace that is heated by a fireplace. That cozy terrace is a wonderful place to spend a rainy evening while enjoying your favorite drinks. In 1969, John Lennon and Yoko Ono stayed at this hotel. Travellers are welcome to book spacious guestrooms designed in Dutch style with all amenities needed for comfortable stay. Breakfasts and dinners are served at award winning Roberto's restaurant that offers delicious Italian cuisine.

Sofitel Legend The Grand Amsterdam

The next hotel, Sofitel Legend The Grand Amsterdam is open in a historic building that was constructed yet in the 15th century and is currently known as a protected site. Initially, the building was used as a monastery and later it was transformed into a municipality. The hotel offers guestrooms of different categories, with historic suites named after different royal guests being the most interesting ones. In different times such noble people as Wilhelm V, Maria de Medici and Willem van

Oranje stayed in those suites. In 1969 the hotel hosted the wedding ceremony of Beatrix, Queen of the Netherlands. There are also three Presidential suites in the hotel that are named after former mayors of Amsterdam Ann Thane, Wim Polak and Ivo Samkalden. The suites were open during a special event in 1992, and all the mayors were present at it. The hotel is proud of its historic past and tries to maintain its highest standards of hospitality, creating pleasant atmosphere for its guests who may feel like royals in this wonderful place.

Waldorf Astoria Amsterdam

A famous hotel, Waldorf Astoria Amsterdam has become a true historic landmark of the city. It is located on the bank of Herengracht Canal that is included in UNESCO World Heritage Site list. The hotel occupies a complex of six unique palaces that date back to the 17th century. The luxurious historic hotel includes 90 guestrooms, each of which is decorated in an unforgettable style with the use of real antiquities.

Besides posh interior and rich history, the hotel is famous for its fine cuisine restaurant Librije's Zusje Amsterdam that is awarded with two Michelin stars.

INK Hotel Amsterdam

One more wonderful and prestigious hotel, INK Hotel Amsterdam is located in a historic building that was the headquarters of De Tijid newspaper around a century ago. Original design is one of the biggest attraction points of the hotel. Thanks to it the hotel won several prestigious awards. The space, which had been once used as a press centre of the newspaper, was transformed into the stylish Pressroom bar. The spacious lounge zone of the hotel is decorated with old issues of the newspaper that date back to 1904. The latest renovation was finished in 2015 at the hotel and it attracted best architects and designers from Europe.

Legendary Hotels

Amsterdam for couples in love - best hotels for intimate escape, wedding or honeymoon

The Toren

The Toren is a wonderful hotel for a romantic vacation in Amsterdam. This hotel has simply everything for an intimate and pleasant holiday. Charming atmosphere, warm and cozy design, ambient lightning in guest rooms and king size beds with heavy baldakins will help hotel guests enjoy one-of-a-kind experience. All guest rooms at the hotel differ in design and size, ranging from small to posh and spacious, so every traveler will easily find a room to fit one's taste. The design of this hotel can be called luxurious, artistic and even slightly mystic. The hotel's staff ensures that guests are satisfied and tries to fulfill all requests of the hotel's customers in a fast and efficient way. The Toren doesn't have its own restaurant, but Christophe' restaurant is located nearby, and guests are welcome to dine there or order in-room service.

Estheréa Hotel

For more than 60 years boutique hotel Estheréa Hotel has been owned and run by the same family. This is a charming and not noisy hotel, where travelers will find luxurious tapestries, bright wallpapers, crystal chandeliers, lots of flowers and exotic fish in the big aquarium in the lobby. The hotel's staff offers premium service and attention to all requests of guests. Free coffee, tea or hot chocolate are always available in the lounge zone, and in the morning travellers are treated with delicious hot breakfast.

Hotel Seven One Seven
Hotel Seven One Seven will be a perfect choice for tourists who value comfort, home-like atmosphere and respect for privacy. All eight guestrooms of the hotel are decorated with paintings, antiquities and precious historic artifacts. The guest rooms are named after Goethe, Shakespeare, Tolkien, List, Schubert, Picasso and Mahler. Large panoramic windows offer stunning views of the city. Breakfasts are served directly in guest rooms or visitors can choose to eat in a cozy inner yard or a lobby. If you would like to stay in a charming romantic place, this wonderful hotel will fulfill your expectations!

Park Hotel

This hotel is located in walking distance from signature landmarks and attractions of Amsterdam. Park Hotel is very popular with couples. The hotel would be a perfect choice for various events and celebrations, as well as a secluded and romantic vacation. Couples can book exclusive rooms with a round shaped bed and luxurious bathroom. The hotel can be proud of its excellent lounge bar and restaurant that specializes in Asian cuisine. The restaurant is decorated in elegant oriental style.

Room Mate Aitana

Opened in 2013, Room Mate Aitana is located in a modern building distinguished by its original design. The hotel is built on a man-made island on the IJ River. Travelers can choose from 280 guest rooms of different type. Designer guest rooms of the hotel are made in bright colors and decorated with elegant fabrics. These romantic guest rooms will be a wonderful choice for couples. The outer wall is replaced with a panoramic window; besides posh rooms, travelers are welcome to use various services offered by Room Mate Aitana. The hotel has its own quay for boats, so vacationers are always welcome to make an entertaining water journey. In the evening, the restaurant that specializes in international cuisine will be the best place for rest. The restaurant's hall offers panoramic views of the river.

Radisson Blu Hotel, Amsterdam

Enjoying a prime location not far away from the heart of the city, Radisson Blu Hotel, Amsterdam, nevertheless, is situated on one of the calmest and picturesque streets of Amsterdam. The hotel is located in a luxurious historic building. Couples can book either standard rooms or exclusive suites. Some guest rooms are made in a sophisticated modern style, while others feature antiquities. Many guest rooms have the original wooden beams. There are a restaurant and a bar at the hotel, but guests will also find many restaurants and shops nearby.

Shopping in Amsterdam

Authentic goods, best outlets, malls and boutiques

Amsterdam is always in the top list of the most popular cities for fans of shopping. Shopaholics arrive to the city from different parts of the world in order to buy unique clothes made of cannabis, luxurious jewelry with diamonds, rare antiquities and original national souvenirs. There are many department stores, outlets, boutiques and markets to fit any taste in Amsterdam. One of the biggest flower markets in the world is also located there.

Famous Flower Market in Amsterdam is located not far away from Singel Canal. A visit to the market will be entertaining not only for professional florists. Everyone is welcome to purchase tulip bulbs, seeds of various flowers and, of course, flowers grown by local florists. Various garden decorations can also be purchased on the market, as well as souvenirs that are usually reasonably priced on the flower market.

Bijenkorf remains the main department store in Amsterdam. It is located in the heart of the city on Dam Square. The store is open in a beautiful historic building. Inside visitors will find shops of internationally famous clothes and accessory brands, jewelry boutiques and electronics shops, as well as several stores that sell elite perfumes. This department store is particularly popular with females as its ground floor is the location of the largest cosmetics shop in the city. Tourists will be interested in attending a wonderful shop that sells Dutch cheese. The shop, which is also located in Bijenkorf, not only sells cheese, but also allows sampling this delicious national product before the purchase.

Travellers, who are not very interested in department stores and malls, may enjoy a walk in De Negen Straatjes quarter. This quarter is located not far away from the central square and consists of nine small streets full of various interesting shops. De Negen Straatjes is famous for the highest concentration of shops in whole Amsterdam. While walking in colorful streets, one will see exclusive designer boutiques, supermarkets with fresh products and bakery, charming bars and shops that sell vintage. Some of the shops are very original and interesting to visit. For example, Brillmuseum the name of this shop can be literally translated as "the museum of spectacles". Unusual and stylish clothes can be found in Goods.

Metz&Co is considered one of the most beautiful shopping centres in Amsterdam. It is located in a beautiful historic building and design of this shopping centre reminds more of a luxurious museum, all exhibits in which can be purchased. Visitors will find in Metz&Co tableware by internationally famous makers, clothes and perfumes of famous brands. However, many tourists visit this shopping centre simply to eat and relax in a café that is located on the sixth floor of the building. Windows of the café provide wonderful views of the central part of Amsterdam and its landmarks.

Tourists, who want to bring exclusive jewelry from Amsterdam, are recommended to head to Coster Diamonds. This is the oldest diamond polishing factory in the city, and it can be visited during an excursion. There is a jewelry shop in the factory, where it is possible to purchase fine jewelry with diamonds and other precious stones. One more pleasant thing prices in that shop are usually relatively cheaper than in many other jewelry stores in the city.

Kalverstraat is usually called the noisiest and most crowded street in Amsterdam. Even budget tourists will enjoy a walk on this street as the majority of shops there have very reasonable prices. There are approximately 120 shops in Kalverstraat, where locals and guests of the city can buy clothes, shoes and accessories. Vast majority of the shops belong to the mass market segment.

The best Amsterdam shopping

Canal Belt - West

The Frozen Fountain

The minimalist interiors that were all the rage a few years back in the Netherlands still have loyal fans, but now there's a quirkier, more colourful and playful touch to edgy Dutch design. The Frozen Fountain brings together hot new local talent and established figures to make exciting chemistry with the occasional art installation or photographic exhibition. There are plenty of smaller, portable objects on sale though you might just be tempted into shipping something big. Seek out salvaged-wood tables and cabinets by Piet Hein Eek or wonderfully abstract carpets by Claudy Jongstra.

Address: Prinsengracht 645

Contact: 00 31 20 622 9375; frozenfountain.nl

Opening times: Mon, 1pm-6pm; Tues-Sat, 10am-6pm; Sun, 12pm-5pm

Prices: Euro

De Kaaskamer

Large wheels of cheese are piled to the ceiling, wedges line the shelves, and a milky aroma fills the air. If you've only ever had the rubbery Dutch cheese exported to supermarkets, you're in for a very different experience. The older cheeses, such as *belegen* (matured for 16-18 weeks) or *oude kaas* (10-12 months), are firm, even crunchy, with a caramel tang. Try the truffle cheese (which tops all for me), or family favourites *nagelkaas* (pitted with cloves), and *komijnekaas* (spiced with cumin). Assistants will slice off slivers for you to taste, and they'll shrink-wrap cheese for you to take home.

Contact: 00 31 20 623 3483; kaaskamer.nl

Opening times: Mon 12pm-6pm; Tue-Fri, 9am-6pm; Sat 9am-5pm; Sun, 12pm-5.00pm

Prices: £

Mint Mini Mall

The ideal 'something for someone who has everything' spot. Mint is a mall in concept, though not in appearance a single shop, long and light with merchandise grouped in different 'departments'. Seek out the cabinet of wooden phone covers, some extremely stylish baby clothes, a cluster of chunky ceramics, and greetings cards impregnated with seeds that grow wildflowers when the card is buried. Originality is the guiding theme, with a nod to natural and sustainable materials. Mint is the place to come if you're buying gifts for both genders and a range of ages, and are in need of inspiration.

Contact: 00 31 20 627 2466; mintminimall.nl

Opening times: Mon, 12.30pm-6pm; Tues-Sat, 10.30am-6pm; Sun, 12.30pm-5pm

Prices: ££

Pontifex

Speciality stores like Pontifex once abounded in the Negen Straatjes quarter, but as the little streets crisscrossing the main canals have become more hip, rents have risen, and shops like this have been squeezed out by boutiques and cafés. Pontifex sells candles. Only candles (well, with a few candlesticks, and some incense). There are candles coloured and plain, patterned and scented, embossed with religious images, and formed into skulls, Buddhas and human torsos. The shop also has an intriguing sideline. The owner is a doll and teddy doctor of note, and he repairs damaged items in his workshop out the back.

Contact: 00 31 20 626 5274

Opening times: Mon-Fri, 10am-6pm; Sat, 10am-5pm

Prices: £

Rinascimento

A tunnel of a shop, stacked floor to ceiling with Delftware both antique and fresh from the kiln. There are plates and urns, tiles and even ornamental clogs, with not only the traditional blue-and-white porcelain from Delft itself, but multi-coloured Makkum china, too. The company packages well, and ships worldwide. For a quintessentially Dutch buy, choose a tulip vase, with individual funnels for single blooms a design dating from the 17th-century tulip mania, when the price of a single bulb could set you back as much as a horse and carriage.

Contact: 00 31 20 622 7509;

Opening times: daily, 9am-6pm

Prices: £££

Sukha Amsterdam

Dutch-designed fashion, footwear, jewellery and accessories produced with an eco-friendly mindset, Sukha is among the new line-up of designer boutiques and high-end delis on Haarlemmerstraat and Haarlemerdijk. With such such a pleasing mix, it is my favourite shopping drag in town. At Sukha, you'll find everything from hefty wooden-bead necklaces and hand-stitched desert boots, to sturdy shopping bags and soft cotton shirts. Keep an eye out for the chunky, hand-knitted woollen scarves, designed by the owner, Irene Mertens, and made by craftswomen in Nepal.

Contact: 00 31 20 330 4001;

Opening times: Mon, 11am-6.30pm; Tues-Sat, 10am-6.30pm; Sun, 12pm-5pm

Prices: ££

Skins

The fragrance world's equivalent of a boutique winery. Ranged on the shelves are scents and bodycare products from exclusive makers, many of them available at only a handful of outlets worldwide. Some come from small, specialist concerns like Biehl Parfumkunstwerke; others from centuries-old masters of the art, such as L. T. Piver, whose aromas wafted through the court of Louis XVI. There are insider names such as local makeup genius Ellen Faas, or Hollywood hair expert Philip B. If you have half-an-hour to spare, go for a digital perfume diagnosis, which hones choices down to one or two.

Contact: 00 31 20 240 0199;

Opening times: Mon-Fri, 10am-7pm; Sat, 10am-6pm; Sun, 12pm-5pm

Prices: £££

Van Ravenstein

Clinically cool, pristine white, with fashion items on display like pieces in a museum Van Ravenstein is the nirvana of cutting-edge Dutch and Belgian design. It's the sort of boutique you feel compelled to dress up for simply to enter, and carry tweezers with you to lift up the clothes. Fashionistas and wealthy women about town come for garments by the likes of Dries van Noten and Viktor & Rolf. If you don't have a few thousand euros to spend, drop by on a Saturday, when there's an outlet section in the basement with more affordable options.

Contact: 00 31 20 639 0067

Opening times: Mon, 1pm-6pm; Tues-Fri, 11am-6pm; Sat, 10.30am-5.30pm

Prices: £££

't Zonnetje

This 'mom-and-pop' coffee shop has been selling teas and coffees for more than 100 years, its big brass dispensers, old-fashioned scales, and time-aged tea caddies still functional and intact. The quarter of town, the Haarlemmerbuurt, is how I remember the Negen Straatjes (the alleys that crisscross the canals) being a decade or so ago, before they became hip and the rents went up. Here you'll still find neighbourhood shops and quirky stores, alongside high-end delis and boutiques. 't Zonnetje stocks more than 25 sorts of tea and over fresh-roast coffees. Try their enticingly mild home blend.

Contact: 00 31 20 623 0058

Opening times: Mon-Fri, 9am-6pm; Sat, 9am-5pm

Prices: £

Canal Belt - East

Amsterdam Vintage Watches

Fancy a 1950s Rolex, or a gleaming gold fob watch? This is the place for that eye-catching vintage timepiece from precision military watches, to complex, multi-faced chronographs. But the reason many people come to the shop is for its parallel line in antique jewellery delicate diamond earrings, an Art Deco brooch, a pearl necklace, cameo rings all selected by a very fine eye. There are collectors' items, but also pieces that are simply beautiful to wear. If your taste is for something more contemporary, don't be put off by the shop's name new Dutch designers get a look in, too.

Contact: 00 31 20 638 0296;

Opening times: Tues-Sat, 10am-6pm; Sun, 1pm-5pm

Prices: £££

Flower Market

Buckets of tulips, banks of brightly coloured blooms, bulbs, pot plants and (increasingly) a cluttering of tourist souvenir paraphernalia line a narrow street. On warm days, mingled scents of flowers waft through the walkway. People jostle to buy bags of tulip bulbs and bouquets of cut flowers, or simply wander from stall to stall, soaking in the ambience. Note that there are strict customs regulations governing the export of bulbs to outside the EU. Many of the bulbs on sale are packaged with an eye to the tourist market.

Opening times: Mon-Sat, 9am-5.30pm; Sun, 11.00am-5.30pm

Prices: £

Anneke Schat

Artist Anneke Schat is also one of the Netherlands' foremost jewellery designers (her patrons include members of the Dutch royal family). Japanese calligraphy, and elements of the natural world especially ones that evoke movement, such as wind and water all form part of the inspiration for her delicate, complex pieces in gold, silver, amber, precious and semi-precious stones. Pieces are distinctive, with a sense of daring. While most of the pieces are in the upper price bracket, you might find the odd more affordable line.

Contact: 00 31 20 625 1608;

Opening times: Thurs-Fri 10am-6pm, Sat 10am-5pm

Prices: £££

Hester Van Eeghen

Discover geometric, daringly coloured bags, briefcases, shoes, and more from local design deity, Hester van Eeghen. Local fashionistas adore her handbags, not only for their stylishness, but for their capacity, strong craftsmanship and practical design. Shape, colour, and surprise are guiding principles in the design, and the products are handcrafted in Milan. Hester travels the world on the lookout for new ideas. Keep an eye open for the one-off special lines that are a by-product of these journeys Cambodian hand-woven silk scarves, perhaps. Her other 'flagship' bag and shoe stores are on Hartenstraat.

Contact: 00 31 20 626 9213

Opening times: Mon, 1pm-6pm; Tues-Sat, 11am-6pm; Sun, 12pm-5pm

Prices: £££

Spiegelkwartier

The Spiegelkwartier arts and antiques district has been going for a good 100 years, brimming with booty of such quality that it can bill itself as a 'supplier to the Rijksmuseum'. The shops are handily located one beside the other on the street that leads up to the museum. You can pick up anything from a Picasso print to period jewellery. Although on the pricey side, with some only enduring the pangs of window shopping, a visit to the Spiegelkwartier doesn't have to bust the bank. An antique Delft tile (from Kramer, or M.C. Gasseling) makes an interesting gift, and is easily transportable home.

Contact:

Opening times: various

Prices: ££-£££

Van Roselen Fine Chocolates

The shop front is so smart you might be tempted to miss it. Inside however, the musty, sweet, comforting aromas of chocolate tell the true story. Van Roselen sells its own handmade, heart-meltingly good chocolates and truffles ranging from classic pralines to curious combinations of fruits and spices. It also stocks prime chocolate from Mexico, Peru, Ecuador and more. A box of their fingertip-sized chocs is an ideal dinner party gift just the right size for two (alright, three) with coffee after a meal.

Contact: 00 31 20 620 2777;

Opening times: Mon-Wed, Fri, Sat 10am-6pm;

Thurs,10am-7pm, Sun 11am-6pm

Prices: ££

Central Amsterdam

By AMFI

Check out who the next hot Dutch fashion designer might be, and pick up an affordable something to wear home. By AMFI is the showcase store for the Amsterdam Fashion Institute, with clothes, accessories and some interiors pieces by teachers and alumni, as well as by current students: from hip T-shirts and suede leather coats to recycled-fabric bags and eyebrow-raising evening dresses. Look for the 'Individuals' label an annual collaboration by all the students on concept, design and fabrics which has come up with some really cool clothes over the years.

Contact: 00 31 20 525 8133

Opening times: Mon-Fri, 1pm-6pm

Prices: ££

Droog

This is the flagship store of the Amsterdam-based design studio, Droog. It's stocked not only with its own stylish homeware, but with clothing and beauty sections too. A collective of different designers, Droog is renowned internationally for sleek, clean designs, often with a dry, witty edge (the name Droog means 'Dry') a doorbell made with inverted wine glasses, a clothes-hanger lamp and folding cutlery that slips into a plastic credit-card holder. Climb the stairs to find the sparkling white, über-cool café overlooking a quiet canal (not many people do).

Contact: 00 31 20 523 5050

Opening times: Daily, 9am-7pm

Prices: £££

Oudemanhuispoort Book Market

Slip through an arched, 18th-century portal in a wall beside the Kloveniersburgwal canal for a second-hand book-buying experience from another era. Men unlock wooden shutters along the bare brick wall of a dim passageway. The shutters flap down as foldable tables, on which are spread collectible books, nondescript dusty tomes, old prints and engravings, and piles of sheet music. Students pass in surges as classes end; the arcade was built as the entrance to an almshouse which now forms part of the University of Amsterdam.

Opening times: Mon-Sat, 9am-5pm

Prices: £

Waterlooplein Flea Market

Once the heart of the Jewish Quarter, this has been the site of market trading for centuries, and today sells everything from mildewy old overcoats and vintage designer classics, to Peruvian jumpers and odd bits of bicycles. Though becoming increasingly commercialised, the flea market is still a fun place to seek out clothing bargains, gifts with a difference, and handmade knick-knacks from around the world. Haggling is not generally the order of the day, but a subtle 'and that's your best price?' may get you places.

Contact:

Opening times: Mon-Sat, 9am-6pm

Prices: £

X Bank

You'll find everything from old-school products (tinned butter, where the label hasn't changed since colonial times) to cutting-edge clothing. Haute couture and off-the-peg line the rails' watches, jewellery, knick-knacks, beauty products, crockery, sculptures and prints stretch through a vast area of varied spaces. There are wacky shoes by Jan Jansen, gilded objets from Marcel Wanders, and vibrantly coloured, beautifully tailored dresses from Matthijs van Bergen. X Bank works as a showcase and forum for local artists and designers in all fields, so there's often something going on: a show, installation, performance or talk.

Contact: 00 31 20 811 3320;

Opening times: Mon-Wed, Fri-Sat, 10am-8pm; Thurs, 10am-9pm; Sun, 12pm-8pm

Prices: ££

Museum District and De Pijp

Albert Cuyp Market

The busy general market in De Pijp runs for over a mile. Between the piles of silk, gaudy modern clothes and cheap shoes, you'll find boxes of dried herbs and teas, people slipping raw herring down their throats (in the time-honoured Dutch way), nibbling on homemade chocolates, tasting farm cheeses, and stocking up on fish, fruit and vegetables for even greater feasting at home. Behind the stalls there's yet another layer of life fabric shops, ethnic stores and cheap Asian and Surinamese eateries. Take a break at one of the pavement cafés along Eerste Van der Helststraat.

Contact:

Opening times: Mon-Sat, 9am-5pm

Prices: £

Oosterdok and Amsterdam East

Pure Market

Food, crafts, artisanal deli goods, beauty products from sustainable sources, a solar-powered carousel all can be found in the Pure Market. Every fortnight this travelling market comes to town, and it's a favourite spot to impress the current house guests. You can sit down to eat with everybody bringing their pick from one of the stalls organic sausages, perhaps, or vegetarian Surinamese roti. There are two main Amsterdam locations: Frankendael Park and Amstel Park. The latter is the one to go for: a vast, beautifully laid-out park on the southern edge of town, with a small lake at the centre.

Contact: I

Opening times: Frankendael Park, last Sun of the month, 11am-6pm, excluding Nov, Jan, Feb; Amstel Park, second Sun of the month, 11am-6pm, excluding Nov, Jan, Feb, Mar; check website for further one-off locations

Prices: £

The Jordaan and Amsterdam West
Chocolátl

Billing itself as a 'chocolate gallery' with artisanal, single-origin chocolates so beautifully displayed, and in such alluring packaging, that it seems a pity to pick one off the shelf. But take the plunge. You'll be rewarded with exquisite bursts of flavour: from the makers El Rey in Venezuela, perhaps, or Marou from Vietnam. Smaller, craft makers are a speciality, and there are various choccie treats made in-house, as well as bonbons from the Belgian chocolatier extraordinaire, Geert Vercruysse. You'll find excellent coffee and gloriously indulgent hot chocolate here too, an ideal hot drink treat after traipsing round the Jordaan.

Contact:

Opening times: Tues-Fri, noon-6.30pm; Sat, 11am-6.30pm; Sun 1pm-5pm

Prices: ££

De Looier Antiques Market

Nondescript doors lead off the street to a warren of walkways lined with stalls selling antiques and curios. The Antiekcentrum Amsterdam (to give it its official name) offers nearly everything from bric-a-brac to cherishable collector rarities. Cheaper stuff books, DVDs, old china and jewellery is laid out on tables; deeper into the market come kiosks and vitrines with silver, Art Deco rarities, icons, paintings and more. This is one of the few markets in Amsterdam that remains open on a Sunday, and it is an enticing place to while away an hour or two on a rainy afternoon.

Contact: 00 31 20 624 9038;

Opening times: Mon, Wed-Fri, 11am-6pm; Sat, Sun, 11am-5pm

Prices: £-££

Noordermarkt

The small square beside the 17th-century Noorderkerk is the scene of a busy farmers' market on Saturdays (fresh oysters shucked while you wait, farm cheeses and the like), and a flea market on Monday mornings, extending along Westerstraat as a *lapjesmarkt* (rag market). Here you'll find textiles by the metre, as well as vintage clothes bargains, in an old-style neighbourhood market atmosphere complete with street organs. Come early for both markets the farmers' market gets really busy after 11 am, and for the best clothing bargains on Monday, arrive at 9 am, or even a little before.

Contact:

Opening times: Farmers' Market, Sat, 9am-5pm; Clothing/textile Market, Mon, 9am-1pm

Prices: £

Mechanisch Speelgoed

Toddlers, squealing delightedly, scrabble about in boxes of plastic animals; dads murmur nostalgically about old toy cars; and mums assist in the blowing of soap bubbles. This quirky shops sells the sorts of toys you probably thought didn't exist anymore those little hand-held windmill sticks, clockwork clowns, kaleidoscopes, enamel beach buckets decorated with shells and rosy-cheeked babes. There's not a battery or electronic screen in sight. Parents do have to be on the ball there's lots to break or knock over, and the shop can get crowded.

Contact: 00 31 20 638 1680;

Opening times: Mon-Fri, 10am-6pm; Sat, 10am-5pm

Prices: £

Het Oud-Hollandsch Snoepwinkeltje

Explore a sweetshop that seems out of a children's story complete with shelves filled with glass jars full of goodies, and a cheery, tubby lady behind the counter. But 'The Old Dutch Tuck Shop' is not only for the kids. The Dutch love their drop (liquorice), and the shop stocks around 60 different sorts, from forest-fruit or honey-flavoured through to three different strengths of 'salty'- the preferred flavour for adults. Lollies, rock, and all manner of gums and mints complete the array. Try a stick of zoethout a wooden twig that tastes sweet when chewed.

Contact: 00 31 20 420 7390;

Opening times: Tues-Sat, 11am-6.30pm

Prices: £

The best Amsterdam nightlife

From the traditional *bruin cafés* still firmly rooted in once-working-class Jordaan to the trendy hipster hotspots of East Amsterdam, the Dutch capital is certainly not short on places to grab a drink or three as might be expected of the city that birthed one of the world's brewing superpowers (Heineken). Naturally, beer is the drink of choice for most Amsterdammers, but you don't have to look to hard to find swish wine bars, bouncing nightclubs, or even little hole-in-the-wall tasting rooms serving jenever the local variety of gin. Here, our Amsterdam expert, Rodney Bolt, picks out his favourite places for a night on the town.

Central Amsterdam

De Dokter

Some say that at just 18 square metres, 'The Doctor' is the smallest pub in Amsterdam. Certainly, it is one of the most venerable, run by six generations of the same family since 1798 a fact emphasised by the rather melodramatic dust and cobwebs on some lampshades and bric-a-brac. Many decades ago a drinking hole for medical students, De Dokter is these days famed for its range of whiskies and both Dutch and Belgian beers. The whisky is very favourably priced the 'whisky of the month' is usually a top-class single malt, for just €4.50 (£4) a glass.

Contact: 00 31 20 626 4427;

Opening times: Wed-Sat, 4pm-1am

Prices: £

5 & 33

A touch of class in a tacky patch of town, providing a retreat from flashing neon lights, snack-bar queues, and the hordes around Central Station. Hip young things sit around the long black bar, amidst chrome and leather, or in banquette nooks. Around a corner is a quieter lounge area (designer chairs, art books on the shelves). Pale, gaudy and sparkly cocktails are consumed by the tinkling glassful. Take your drink and wander down the stairs to the back of the bar, where you'll find a basement gallery showing edgy contemporary Dutch art.

Contact: 00 31 20 820 5333;

Opening times: Mon-Thurs, 6.30am-1am; Fri-Sun, 6.30am-2am

Prices: ££

Bierfabriek

A cavernous, multi-roomed microbrewery, all scrubbed wood and bare surfaces, which packs out with students, visiting backpackers, and twenty- and thirty-somethings still up for a good time. Beer flows freely, noise levels are high, and a party atmosphere pervades. The brewery makes a toasty porter and a fruity red ale, but I prefer their Puur, a rich, unfiltered yeasty pilsener. They bake their own bread, using brewer's yeast, and turn out plenty of organic grilled chicken to line those empty stomachs. If you're with a group of friends, book a taptafel a table with a private draft pump.

Contact: 00 31 20 528 9910

Opening times: Mon-Thurs, 3pm-1am; Fri, 3pm-2am; Sat, 1pm-2am; Sun, 1pm-midnight

Prices: ££

Café Droog

Dutch design marvel Droog has an extremely cool café above the company shop. It is sparkling white, dotted with furniture, objets d'art, prototypes and leftovers by Droog collaborators. I particularly like Tejo Remy's bundled-up Rag Chair, and Rachel Harding's dinky Chinese restaurant interior constructed in a fish tank. Design aficionados and the severely chic come to snack and sip on juices (think fennel, celery, lime, and cucumber combo). But not that many people wander upstairs from the Droog emporium, so this makes a welcome quiet spot in a hectic part of town, with a few window tables giving a canal view.

Contact: 00 31 20 217 0100;

Opening times: daily 9am-7pm

Prices: ££

De Engelse Reet

There is no bar at De Engelse Reet. Drinks are dispensed in a small backroom, opening into a voorkamer ('front room' or parlour). It's a centuries-old set-up which, as far as I know, remains nowhere else in town. The current owners have run the bar for four generations, and successive first sons have all had the same name. I love the fact that the barman has been called 'Teun van Veen' for more than 85 years. Try one of the jenevers (Dutch gin) from local distillery De Ooievaar, which dates back to 1782 they have a really good range here.

Contact: 00 31 20 623 1777

Opening times: Mon-Thurs, 12pm-1am; Fri, Sat, 12pm-2am

Prices: £

Grand Café 1e Klas

The former first-class waiting room at Central Station appears with every bit of its original grandeur high ceilings, large Delft vases, potted palms, William Morris patterns on the walls and rafters (and these days a grumpy resident cockatoo). The station was designed in 1882, as a palatial paean to the new railways. First-class passengers were given royal treatment, and it shows. This is an ideal spot to meet up with someone if one of you doesn't know the city, though you may have to pick up a (free) platform access ticket to do so. It's easy to find, directly on the station platform (but be careful not to confuse it with Pub 1e Klas next door).

Contact: 00 31 20 625 0131;

Opening times: daily, 8.30am-11pm

Prices: £

Hoppe

A reproduction Old Master on the wall, fine sand on the wooden floor, barrels behind the bar Hoppe is every inch a traditional 'brown café' (so named for the wood panelling and eons of tobacco smoke staining walls and ceiling). Hoppe has been going strong since 1670 the right-hand part, the 'Standing Room', is the oldest. For decades it was an establishment place, as opposed to the more bohemian Café De Zwart across the alley, and in a way the division still holds true. Avoid coming in the early evening, when Hoppe becomes unbearably packed with after-work drinkers in suits.

Contact: 00 31 20 420 4420;

Opening times: Mon-Thurs, 8am-1am; Fri, Sat 8am-2am

Prices: £

Café in De Waag

Built in 1488 as one of Amsterdam's city gates, and transformed in the 17th century into a public weigh-house, 'De Waag' is now a café and restaurant. Inside, it's all bare brick and burnished wood, lit by nearly 300 candles. Boy, can that make it hot in summer! But then there's a neatly enclosed terrace outside the main door, with a view onto the hurly-burly of Nieuwmarkt square, on the edge of the Red Light District. This is a good place to come if you want a drink in a more sedate atmosphere than most other cafés in the quarter offer.

Contact: 00 31 20 422 7772;

Opening times: Mon-Wed, 11am-10.30pm; Thurs-Sun, 9am-10.30pm

Prices: ££

De Jaren

White walls, light woods, high ceilings and minimalist design combine with huge windows overlooking the Amstel River, and a terrace jutting out over the water. De Jaren is a longstanding networking venue for arts and media folk, and heaves at cocktail hour, but I love it most on a sunny day, when you can moor a boat alongside for a drink on the terrace. It's also great for whiling away a rainy afternoon, in a basket chair or at the long reading table. Upstairs, in the evenings, there's a well-stocked salad bar (rare in Amsterdam), as well as affordable fuller meals.

Contact:00 31 20 625 5771;

Opening times: Sun-Thurs, 8.30am-1am; Fri, Sat 8.30am-2am

Prices: ££

Café Van Zuylen

A down-to-earth 'brown café' (bars named for their traditional wooden interiors, and tobacco-smoke-stained walls). One room, especially in the evenings, is cheerfully noisy, and crammed shoulder-to-shoulder. Another reached through a door beside the bar, or via a separate street entrance sports a chandelier and paintings on the wall, and tends to be a little quieter and better suited to couples. In good weather, tables and basket-chairs are spread out on an enormous terrace, which stretches across a bridge over the Singel canal an ideal spot to lean back and bask in the sun for a while.

Contact: 00 31 20 639 1055

Opening times: Sun-Thu, 10am-1am; Fri, Sat, 10am-3am

Prices: £

Wynand Fockink

Yes, the name is for real, and perfectly polite. Wynand Fockink is the man who first opened this distillery and proeflokaal (tasting room) in 1679. The distillery still produces fine liqueurs and jenever (Dutch gin), and the proeflokaal remains pretty much unaltered after more than three centuries: wood-panelled, sawdust on the floor, shelves lined with bottles of quaintly named liqueurs. It's teeny, and packs out in the early evenings (though a quick late-afternoon shot does wonders on an icy winter's day). If you've only ever tried sharp-tasting commercial Dutch jenevers, treat yourself here to a Superior three-year-old malt.

Contact: 00 31 20 639 2695;

Opening times: daily, 2pm-9pm

Prices: £

Canal Belt West

De Melkweg

Still going strong since the heady 1970s, when it was at the heart of European counter-culture, the 'Milky Way' is a cutting-edge music and performance venue, and hosts wild weekend club nights. The original old dairy building has been expanded with flash new extensions to include a cinema, art gallery and café, hosting everything from Dutch pop via grunge rock and hiphop to contemporary dance. Perhaps as a hangover from the Flower Power days, when De Melkweg was the scene of the first public puffs of marijuana, you have to become a member (€4/£3 a month) to get in to most events. Booking ahead is recommended for some events there may be a pre-booking surcharge.

Contact: 00 31 20 531 8181;

Opening times: hours vary according to events

Prices: £

Morlang

A two-tier canal-side café that's a perennial favourite with a mixed, thirty-something crowd (the age range edging upwards as the years go by), local office workers loosening their ties and kicking off their heels, and passing visitors. The café buzzes night and day. In good weather there are tables outside, directly beside the canal (though with trams and traffic nearby, it's not the most sedate of spots). In the upstairs room, there's a cosy window nook with a view over the canal, where I'm happy to hole up for hours on a rainy afternoon.

Contact: 00 31 20 625 2681;

Opening times: Sun-Thurs, 11am-1am; Fri, Sat, 11am-2am

Prices: ££

Museum District and De Pijp

Flamingo

An upbeat little café at the hub of De Pijp life. It's bang on the Albert Cuyp Market, with fruit boxes stacked beside the terrace, and also on one of the most popular streets for evening revels. They serve mulled wine in the winter, zingy summer mojitos, and a healthy range of beers from ace local brewery, Brouwerij 't IJ. Flamingo makes a good starting point for exploring De Pijp nightlife there are at least ten other bars within a few minutes' walk, and you can sit and survey who is going where, and what's going on.

Contact: 00 31 20 670 9007;

Opening times: Sun-Thu, 10am-1am; Fri, Sat, 10am-

3am

Prices: £

Kingfisher

Budding writers and artists from the neighbourhood, students, and the young and easy-going from around the world hang out, meet up, and have a good time here. A corner café in the heart of De Pijp, Kingfisher is something of a non-Establishment institution (if you'll allow the oxymoron). It's simple inside wooden tables, bentwood chairs, one bright red wall to liven things up and open day and night. During the day, it's great for a quiet coffee; later on, music levels are upped and the Kingfisher hops. Cheap, daily dinner specials are chalked up on a blackboard.

Contact: 00 31 20 671 2395;

Opening times: Mon-Thurs, 10am-1am; Fri, Sat, 10am-3am; Sun, 12pm-1am

Prices: ££

Jordaan and Amsterdam West

Rooie Nelis

A last taste of the old, working-class Jordaan, which has survived the gentrification of the rest of the quarter. Rooie Nelis (Red Nelis) founded the café in 1937, his daughter Blonde Sien, now in her eighties, still holds the reins. Local singers such as Willy Alberti and Johnny Jordaan were regulars here, and went on to become famous throughout the land. Photos and memorabilia cover the walls (Queen Beatrix visited once or twice), you'll probably still find Blonde Sien sitting at the bar, and stalwart, old-style Jordaaners having a drink. Drop in after dinner and you might catch a spontaneous sing-a-long.

Contact: 00 31 20 624 4167

Opening times: Mon-Thurs, 2pm-1am; Fri, Sat, 2pm-2am; Sun, 2pm-midnight

Prices: £

De Tuin

A friendly, down-to-earth Jordaan bar, populated mainly by regulars and folk from the neighbourhood.

De Tuin is my favourite drinking spot in the quarter especially if I can get a seat outside, watching the world go by. Inside it is stone floors, wooden chairs, flowery wallpaper that is retro by default rather than intention, and a delightfully unrelated clutter of prints and pictures. There are eight beers on tap, more bottled, and the wine is palatable. Try one of the Texels beers, from a craft brewery on one of the northern Frisian islands.

Contact:00 31 20 624 4559

Opening times: Mon-Thurs, 10am-1am; Fri, Sat, 10am-3am; Sun, 11am-1am

Prices: £

Oosterdok and Amsterdam East

Bar Bukowski/Henry's Bar

Named after the writer, poet and all-round renegade Charles Bukowski, and with a giant typewriter-key light installation above the bar, this is a young, noisy, friendly place, with people packed in shoulder-to-shoulder most nights, and music the whole merrily along. But I prefer the slightly more subdued Henry's Bar, through an archway, where there are scatterings of soft chairs, and inspired bartenders create superb cocktails, from classics to the ginger-and-chilli-zapped 'Bar Bukow'. Contrary to the Bukowksi spirit, there's a really good selection of soft drinks for grown ups,including pine-flavoured options.

Contact: 00 31 20 370 1685;

Opening times: Bar Bukowski: Mon-Thurs, 8am-1am; Fri, 8am-3am; Sat, 9am-3am; Sun, 9am-1am. Henry's Bar: Thurs, 8pm-1am; Fri, 6pm-3am; Sat, 8pm-3am

Prices: ££

Hannekes Boom

On one side, wheels screech on rail tracks, as trains build up speed leaving Central Station. On the other, across the waters of the eastern docks, Renzo Piano's copper-clad NEMO building seems to bear down on you like a giant ocean liner. Hannekes Boom is on a spot of forgotten land, a little lost island with one of the most extraordinary views in town. The shack-like building, with big terraces and tables set out under the trees, attracts a young, alternative crowd and frequently stages live music (funk, jazz, singer songwriters) and arts events. My favourite winter spot? Inside, beside the open hearth.

Contact: 00 31 20 419 9820;

Opening times: Mon-Thurs, 11am-1am; Fri-Sat, 11am-3am

Prices: ££

De Ysbreeker

Design aficionados and lovers of good style (and during the day, their children, too) join passing politicians and the odd recognisable media face in this vast, high-ceilinged café, whose monumental windows overlook the River Amstel. De Ysbreeker dates back to the 18th century and has been an inn, a renowned billiards bar, and a contemporary music venue. Local design guru Ronald Hooft has given the café a sleek makeover, propelling it into the 21st century while keeping original features such as moulded cast-iron pillars. The large, shaded terrace, directly on the river, makes this a great retreat on a hot afternoon.

Contact: 00 31 20 468 1808;

Opening times: Sun-Thurs, 8am-1am; Fri, Sat 8am-2am

Prices: ££

Architecture & monuments

Top architectural sightseeing and landmarks of Amsterdam - ideas on city exploration routes

Of course, in order to feel the magnificent atmosphere of Amsterdam, one needs to visit this place, walk on charming streets of the historical center, visit local cafes, and enjoy the look of the local landmarks - Oude Kerk, Montelbaanstoren, Waag, Magna Plaza, Noorderkerk and many others. In order to make your virtual tour to the city more interactive, we offer an unusual opportunity to fly over every notable landmark of Amsterdam. Simply turn the video on, and use the full-screen feature. Each landmark comes with extra information, containing a collection of interesting facts and a photo gallery. Let's go!

Oude Kerk, Amsterdam
Facts:

» The 800-year-old Gothic church of Oude Kerk is the oldest building in Amsterdam and the old parish church founded approximately in 1306.

» In the 17th century the church became a place of marriage. The shrine was also used as the city archives.

» The remains of the famous Dutch composer, Jan Pieterszoon Sweelinck, which has long been the young organist at Oude Kerk, lie there.

» Rembrandt was a frequent visitor of the church, and all of his children were baptized in the Oude Kerk. A small exhibition of his works has survived in the shrine.

» Floor of the church consists entirely of gravestones. The fact is that the church was built on the site of the cemetery. Locals are still buried at the site within the boundaries of the shrine.

Montelbaanstoren, Amsterdam

Facts:

» Montelbaanstoren is one of the defensive towers of Amsterdam, built in 1512.

» The tower is quite an interesting structure, as its massive bottom is crowned with a white colonnade with a clock.

» Due that clock people unsightly called the tower Silly Jacob, because the clock on the tower showed the wrong time.

» The tower entered the history of world art, as it can be seen at View of the Montelbaanstoren by Rembrandt.

Waag, Amsterdam
Facts:

» Waag is the oldest secular building in Amsterdam constructed in 1488 as the gate of the city wall.

» In the 17th century weighing service (hence the name of the construction) was started in the building; the main task of it was to weigh the goods for the market.

» At that time a few guilds - blacksmiths, painters, masons and surgeons were situated at the upper floors of the building.

» Then the building was used as a fire station, and later as the city archive of Amsterdam.

» Most of the 20th century Waag was working as a museum. Currently, the lower floors of the building are occupied with cafes and restaurants, and the organization working in the field of media technologies occupies the top floor.

Magna Plaza, Amsterdam
Facts:

» The Magna Plaza is the huge shopping center located in the heart of Amsterdam.

» In 1992, the municipality had decided to add a building to the list of the ten most important monuments of Amsterdam.

» In fact, the building occupied by the shopping center originally served as the main post office.

» The building was designed in the neo-Gothic style in

the 19th century by the famous architect Cornelius Hendrik Peters.

» You can find all the well-known global fashion brands, as well as two amazing interior design shop, several souvenir departments, a shop with wooden toys and a shop for skateboarders on three floors of the Magna Plaza.

» The shopping center also has a cozy restaurant and a coffee bar.

Noorderkerk, Amsterdam
Facts:

» Norderkerk or the Northen Church almost hasn't changed over time. It was built in 1623 for the poor.

» The church is designed in form of the equilateral Greek cross, which was an innovation for its time.

» At the entrance to the church there is the sculpture consisting of three connected pieces, which is dedicated to popular clamor. There is the inscription on it, telling 'The Power - in solidarity.'

» In 1627 the square around Nordekerk has become a

place for selling pans, pots and used clothing. The tradition continues even these days; currently there is a flea market there.

Tropenmuseum, Amsterdam
Facts:

» The Tropenmuseum is the major ethnographic museum in Amsterdam.

» The museum is one of the leading venues in Europe, which is famous for its rich collections.

» Eight permanent and a series of temporary exhibitions, including collection of both modern and traditional fine art and collection of photographs, are represented in the museum.

» There you can see life in tropical and subtropical regions of the world: India, Southeast Asia and South America. The museum thoroughly recreates flavor of these places, so you can see the huts of the natives, bazaars and more; even the local smells and sounds are reproduced here.

» The museum has its own theater, where concerts of

Eastern music, theater and dance performances are held every evening.

Science Center Nemo, Amsterdam
Facts:

» The Nemo Center is the largest science museum in the Netherlands. It attracts more than 500,000 visitors annually, making it the fifth most visited museum in the country.

» The construction of this large research center resembles a huge green ship in five floors. Thanks to the architect's plan, inside the museum you can see the vent pipes, steel slabs and other functional parts of the building.

» On the first floor you can enjoy half-hour show representing a long chain reaction, and the second floor houses the ball factory.

» There is the scientific laboratory on the third floor, where people can conduct scientific experiments; there is a section dedicated to the human brain on the fourth floor. Here you can explore the memory, the brain and senses.

» The roof of the museum is looking over the old town. This is the only place in Amsterdam, which offers such a great view.

Excursion tour in Amsterdam.

Top architecture - monuments, castles, temples and palaces

Let's move further. The upcoming famous architecture monuments of Amsterdam that deserve to be mentioned are Royal Palace, Westerkerk, National Monument, State Museum, Church of St. Nicholas, South Church, and Beurs van Berlage. An overview of interesting facts and a collection of photographs are available for each monument. In order to plan a route for your real-life sightseeing tour in Amsterdam, use our interactive map of sights in of Amsterdam that is available below this article.

Royal Palace, Amsterdam

» The Royal Palace is one of the three palaces in the Netherlands at the disposal of the monarch.

» The palace has been built to serve as a town hall in the Golden Age. Later, the building became the royal palace of King Louis Napoleon, and later it was converted into the Dutch royal palace.

» At present, the venue is used by the monarch for entertaining and formal events. New Year's court is annually held there.

» Numerous halls and galleries of the royal palace are adorned with paintings by Dutch artists, including Rembrandt, Govert Flinck, Jacob Jordaens, Jan Lievens and Ferdinand Bol.

» Rembrandt completed his largest canvas, The Conspiracy of Claudius Civilis, for the new Town Hall.

Westerkerk, Amsterdam

Facts:

» Westerkerk was one of the first purpose-built Protestant churches in Amsterdam.

» Today Westerkerk is the largest Calvinist church in

the Netherlands.

» Approximately in 1669, the great Rembrandt was buried at the north wall of Westerkerk.

» The spire of the temple is the tallest church spire in Amsterdam; its height is 85 meters.

» Westerkerk is located very close to the Anne Frank House, where during World War II the Jewish girl Anne, her family and friends have being hid from Nazi persecution for two years. Westerkerk is often mentioned in her diary, as its clock tower is visible from the attic of the house, where the girl was hiding. Now, there is the statue of Anne Frank on the church square.

National Monument, Amsterdam

Facts:

» The National Monument is the memorial in Amsterdam commemorating victims of World War II.

» Annually on May 4 the memorial ceremony is held in memory of those killed during the WWII and the subsequent armed conflict.

» The central part of the monument is a 22-meter column-cone. Four chained male figures of the monument symbolize the suffering during the war.

» Two more figures, symbols of the clerisy (left) and working class (right) united into a single cohesive resistance are seen on both sides of the monument. A dog howling at their feet symbolizes the pain and dedication.

» Above the central bas-relief of the memorial there is a sculpture of a woman with a child and pigeons around them; that's a symbol of victory, peace, and a new life. Doves are the symbol of liberation from the yoke of Nazism.

State Museum, Amsterdam

Facts:

» The State Museum is the Dutch national museum dedicated to the art and history. The museum is located on the Museum Square in Amsterdam near the Van Gogh Museum.

» In 2013, the State Museum became the most visited

museum in the Netherlands, with a record number of 2.2 million visitors.

» The museum has a collection of art (paintings, sculptures and decorative arts, the art of Asia), a collection of historical items (archaeological artifacts, paintings, sculptures, clothing) and a collection of drawings, prints and photographs.

» In total, the museum displays about 8,000 works of art and history. The total number of exhibits is more than one million.

» The art collection is based on numerous works by Dutch masters of 15-19th centuries, in particular, the famous masters of the 17th century. The most notable are Rembrandt, Vermeer and Hals, as well as de Hooch, Steen, Ruisdael van der Gelst, van Scorel and others.

Church of St. Nicholas, Amsterdam

Facts:

» The Church of St. Nicholas is the largest Catholic church in Amsterdam.

» The special niche in the top of the gable houses the

statue of the patron saint of the church and the city, St. Nicholas. St. Nicholas is also the patron saint of travelers, merchants and sailors.

» Recently the church has been completely renovated; inside the church there is a fully functioning organ dating back to the 19th century. Organ concerts are held there from time to time.

» The church is decorated with two majestic towers; between them there is rose-like window depicting Jesus and the four Evangelists.

» The church has cross-like shape with three outbuildings.

South Church, Amsterdam

Facts:

» Construction of the South Church was completed in 1611. This temple was the first in Amsterdam, which was built specifically for the Protestants.

» History of the South Church is closely associated with life of Rembrandt, whose house was situated nearby. Three children of the artist were buried in this church.

» Rembrandt wrote the famous painting, Night Watch, in this church, as his workshop was too small for that.

» In summer for a small fee you can climb the 70-meter bell tower of the church offering spectacular panorama of the city.

» Currently, the church is a tourist landmark. After restoration of the temple, liturgy is no longer held there. The room of the shrine is now used for temporary exhibitions.

Beurs van Berlage, Amsterdam

Facts:

» Beurs van Berlage is considered to be the most interesting architectural monument of the Netherlands dating back to the 19th century.

» Berlage Stock Exchange was built from 1898 to 1903. The building housed several different exchanges, including stock, grain, currency and freight.

» Beurs van Berlage is decorated with three statues: the statue of the legendary founder of Amsterdam, knight Gijsbrecht van Aemstel, the statue of Admiral and the conqueror of the 17th century, Jan Peterson Kuhn, and the statue of Hugo Grotius, who was the famous Dutch jurist and statesman.

» Currently the exchange building is open to the public as the museum that represents the history of Beurs van Berlage.

Best Things to do in Amsterdam

Amsterdam offers a lot more than vice. There's the world-class Van Gogh Museum, the Rijksmuseum and shopping on Nine Little Streets for culture hounds. Those traveling with kids might enjoy a visit to the Vondelpark and the NEMO Science Museum, a family bike ride or an introduction to Amsterdam's love of pancakes. But of course, the party scene of coffee houses, gay bars, nightclubs and more is not to be missed

Vondelpark

Located southwest of the city center, the 116-acre Vondelpark is the favorite leafy retreat of just about everyone. Not only is it the largest city park in Amsterdam, it's also one of the most revered in all of the Netherlands. Most recent travelers said they enjoyed people-watching and picnicking at the park, but other reviewers recommend avoiding a late-night visit as the park can be a little frightening once the sun sets. During the day, though, the park is filled with couples, families and friends, and is definitely worth a visit.

Ponds, fields and playgrounds are connected by winding paths, which also run by an open-air theater, a rollerblade rental, a rose garden, several cafes and a range of statues and sculptures. Open dawn to dusk, you can take trams 1, 2 or 5 to the Leidseplein, and you'll have just a quick two-minute walk to reach the park's entrance. The park is free to visit.

Vondelpark 1 1071 Amsterdam, Netherlands

Anne Frank House (Anne Frank Huis)

Inside the Anne Frank House, travelers will see the location where not so long ago the 15-year-old Anne Frank penned a journal that would become a best-seller. Travelers can imagine what it'd be like to stay hidden away for more than two years, only to be betrayed and taken to a concentration camp. Artifacts inside the museum include historical documents, photographs, film images and belongings from those in hiding and those who assisted them. Frank's original diary and other notebooks are also on display, though original objects from the annex are not on display, as it was stripped of its contents during the war. A free audio guide available in nine languages is included with admission.

Visitors described the experience as educational but emotional, despite the relatively short time it takes to tour the house (about an hour). Travelers also said that there are most always heavy crowds and long lines, so you'll want to plan ahead.

The Anne Frank House is open daily from 9 a.m. to 10 p.m. April 1 through the end of October and from 9 a.m. to 7 p.m. Nov. 1 through the end of March, with extended hours (until 10 p.m.) on Saturdays. Admission costs 9 euros (about $11) for adults and 4.50 euros (about $5) for children ages 10 to 17; add on an extra half-euro for online ticket purchases (which are required at this time).

If you'd like to enjoy a 30-minute introduction to the life story of Anne Frank, you can book an introductory program ticket, which costs 14.50 euros (almost $18) for adults and 10 euros (almost $12.50) for children ages 10 to 17 (and includes admittance into the house). Keep in mind that demand for tickets almost always exceeds supply. Visitors should also note that until July 1, 2018, tickets can only be purchased online. On-site facilities include a museum store and cafe. You can reach the museum via trams 13, 14 and 17 to the Westermarkt stop. The museum sits about a 20-minute walk from Centraal station. Keep in mind: Photography is not allowed in the museum. For more information, *Prinsengracht 263-267 1016 GV Amsterdam, Netherlands*

Verzetsmuseum (Dutch Resistance Museum)

The Verzetsmuseum (the Dutch Resistance Museum), located by the Artis Royal Zoo, has been called the city's best-kept secret by some. The informative even inspiring museum tells the stories of those who lived in the Netherlands during the Nazi occupation and explains how the atrocities of World War II transpired. Through authentic objects, photos and documents, film and sound fragments, visitors will learn how the resistance manifested in the Netherlands.

Recent travelers said the thought-provoking museum leads you to ask yourself what you would've done during the Nazi occupation of your country. They were also pleased with the audio guides that are given with the ticket price, as well as with the exhibits which are translated into both Dutch and English.

The museum is open Monday through Friday from 10 a.m. to 5 p.m. and Saturday through Sunday from 11 a.m. to 5 p.m. Recent visitors hailed this museum's reasonable admission price: 11 euros for adults (about $13.50) and 6 euros (approximately $7.50) for children ages 7 to 15. If you purchased an I amsterdam City Card, your entry is covered. The museum also contains a restaurant and a gift shop. To get here, take the 9 or 14 tram to the Artis Zoo, Plantage Kerklaan or Plantage Middenlaan/Kerklaan stops. The museum is about a 30-minute walk from the Anne Frank House, if you're hoping to combine a visit to both.

Van Gogh Museum

The Van Gogh Museum holds the world's largest collection of Van Gogh's paintings and drawings, including "Sunflowers" and "Almond Blossom." The museum itself regularly tops the list as the most-visited museum in not only Amsterdam but in all of the Netherlands, as travelers come from near and far to see the artworks created by the tortured artist, who cut off his own ear and committed suicide at the rise of his success.

Because of Van Gogh's popularity, some travelers highly recommend purchasing online tickets ahead of time to avoid lengthy museum lines. Others advise visiting on the museum's late Fridays (when the building stays open until 9 p.m.) for ambient music and drinks. Though some were disappointed that the museum does not house some of the artist's more famous paintings (many of them are featured in other museums across the globe), reviewers did praise the museum's layout and its display of his earliest works.

The museum is open Sunday through Thursday from 9 a.m. to 7 p.m., Friday from 9 a.m. to 9 p.m. and Saturday from 9 a.m. to 6 p.m. The admission price is a bit steep, though fans of the tortured artist think the 200 paintings on view are worth it. Adults can get a ticket for 18 euros (about $22). Tack on an extra 5 euros (about $6) if you'd like an audio guide to accompany your visit. If you purchased an I amsterdam City Card, your entry fee is waived. To get to the museum, take either the 2 or 5 tram to the Van Baerlestraat stop, or the 12 tram to the Museumplein stop. Buses No. 347 and No. 357 at the Rijksmuseum or Museumplein stops will also get you there.

Museumplein 6 1071 DJ Amsterdam, Netherlands

Leidseplein

If you're looking for a tamer alternative to Amsterdam's Red Light District, Leidseplein or Leiden Square, may be for you. The center of Amsterdam's entertainment scene, Leidseplein sits southwest of the city center and is filled with nightclubs, movie theaters, concert venues, casinos and, of course, some coffee shops. For the performing arts, the Melkweg (Milky Way) concert hall and the hotel or hostel here or maybe head to the nearby Vondelpark instead.

Travelers were also pleasantly surprised by the quantity and variety of restaurants huddled in the neighborhood, though they do warn of high prices at the bars.

Leidseplein is accessible via the 1, 2, 5, 7 and 10 tram routes via the Leidseplein stop.

Leidseplein 1 Amsterdam

De Pijp

De Pijp, which is also called the Latin Quarter, is known for its 19th-century architecture and its collision of different cultures. Here, you'll find ethnic restaurants, eclectic shops and the tranquil Sarphatipark. The Heineken Experience sits on the northern edge of the neighborhood. Travelers say that De Pijp feels less touristy and more like authentic Amsterdam. They also call it the heart of the city for young people thanks to its beatnik vibe and trendy eateries.

You'll also find the famous street market, Albert Cuyp Market, here Mondays through Saturdays. To start wandering, you might want to find Gerard Douplein square on your Amsterdam map, hitting a cafe and starting your meanderings from there. You can also take either the 3, 4, 12, 16 or 24 tram to reach this happenin' neighborhood, or just walk about a mile south of the city center.

De Negen Straatjes (Nine Little Streets)

De Negen Straatjes, or the Nine Little Streets, are exactly that nine streets that run between the Prinsengracht and Singel canals and are lined with shops and boutiques. (For your orientation, the Singel is the first main canal that wraps around the city center.) Vintage clothing shops nestle alongside accessories stores and interior design boutiques, and hours vary by store.

Recent travelers called the area a lovely place to stroll and said it was less touristy than other parts of the city. Though you'll likely rub elbows with plenty of other travelers, you'll also encounter your fair share of locals.

When your feet get tired, you can take a break from shopping and pop into either Nielsen cafe for an apple tart or the Pompadour for some homemade chocolate two stops recommended by past visitors.

Rijksmuseum (State Museum)

Considered one of Amsterdam's top museums (along with the Van Gogh and Anne Frank museums), the *Rijksmuseum* (or State Museum) features an impressive collection of artists, including Rembrandt and Vermeer. As befits a state museum, the ornate building contains mostly Dutch works from the 15th to 17th centuries though its entire collection stretches across 800 years.

Visitors recommend getting to the Rijksmuseum as early as possible in the day to avoid standing in a line to enjoy both the breathtaking building, grounds and art. According to the museum, the busiest times are Friday, Saturday and Sunday between 11 a.m. and 3 p.m. And once you've finished touring the interior, step outside and enjoy the gardens a recommendation from past visitors. Though some reviewers griped about the museum's confusing layout, they still said it was among their top to-dos in Amsterdam.

To visit, take the 2 or 5 tram to the Rijksmuseum stop, the 7 or 10 tram to the Spiegelgracht stop or the 12 tram to the Museumplein stop. You can visit the museum every day from 9 a.m. to 5 p.m.; tickets cost 17.50 euros for adults (about $22); visitors ages 18 and younger can visit for free. If you purchased an I amsterdam City Card, your admission fee is covered. The Rijksmusuem also contains gardens, a shop, and cafe and those are open to the public without a ticket, but keep in mind that those close one hour later at 6 p.m.

Museumstraat 1 1071 XX Amsterdam, Netherlands

Artis Royal Zoo (Natura Artis Magistra)

Visitors traveling with children in tow might want to make some space in their itinerary for the Artis Royal

Zoo. Lions, monkeys and penguins are housed here, along with about another 750 species, and there's also an aquarium, an insectarium, a butterfly garden and a planetarium.

Although most recent visitors described the zoo as lovely, well maintained and a great family day, some of them concede that enclosures for the animals seemed a bit small.

Adult admission for anyone ages 10 and older costs 23 euros (about $28), and tickets costs 19.50 euros (about $24) for kids ages 3 to 9. If you purchase your tickets ahead of time online, you'll save a few euros. If you purchased the I amsterdam City Card, your entry fee is waived. Guided tours are available very Saturday and Sunday at 2 p.m. The zoo is open daily, but hours vary by the season. Generally, it welcomes visitors from 9 a.m. to 5 or 6 p.m. Every Saturday in June, July and August, the zoo stays open until sunset. To get there, visitors can take the 9 and 14 tram to the Artis stop. The nearest metro station is Waterlooplein.

Plantage Kerklaan 38-40 1018 CZ Amsterdam, Netherlands

Heineken Experience

The Heineken Experience, which takes place in the old *Heineken Brouwerij* (Heineken Brewery), is a must-do for fans of the fermented beverage. And according to its website, the Heineken Experience will dip visitors "chin deep" into the popular beer. Among the attractions housed in the century-old factory are a virtual-reality ride, a history of the Heineken family and a free beer tasting. A downloadable app takes visitors on a historical journey through the factory (available for iPhones and Androids). You should note that only those 18 and older are able to partake in the tasting.

Although some recent travelers highly recommend taking the tour at the Heineken experience, others described it as a marketing ploy rather than a tutorial in the beer-brewing process (the real brewery used for production sits on the outskirts of Amsterdam; this location is simply a museum).

The brewery is open daily (Monday through Thursday from 10:30 a.m. to 7:30 p.m. and Friday through Sunday from 10:30 a.m. to 9 p.m.); during July and August, the Heineken Experience is open every day from 10:30 a.m. to 9 p.m. Adult tickets cost 18 euros (about $22.25). Tickets for kids (ages 12 to 17) cost 14.50 euros (about $18); children ages 11 and younger are admitted for free (keep in mind children are only allowed to enter with an adult and are not served any alcohol). The Heineken Experience is accessible via the 7, 10 and 24 tram routes, and indoor parking is available nearby.

Stadhouderskade 78 1072 AE Amsterdam, Netherlands

Concertgebouw

Constructed in 1888, the *Concertgebouw* (literally Concert Building) hosts 900-plus shows and about 700,000 visitors per year, which makes it one of the world's busiest concert venues. Check the Concertgebouw's website for a list of orchestral and other performances, as well as for ticket prices, which vary by show. From time to time, the venue also offers free lunchtime performances.

Recent visitors called this one of the world's best concert halls, which offers fairly reasonable ticket prices. If you're hoping to attend one of the venue's free concerts, plan to arrive early past visitors said the staff at Concertgebouw hands out tickets on a first-come, first-served basis.

If you're visiting Amsterdam in July or August, you might be able to score some great performances for cheaper prices (around 26 euros, about $32) as part of the annual Robeco Summer Concerts series, which features more than 80 summer concerts. For 10 euros ($12.30), visitors can also take a 75-minute guided tour of the Concertgebouw.

Concertgebouwplein 10 1071 LN Amsterdam, Netherlands

NEMO Science Museum

Anyone that says Amsterdam isn't for kids hasn't visited the NEMO Science Museum, housed inside the ship-like green building on the harbor. Filled with hands-on activities, kids can spend hours concocting chemistry experiences and constructing buildings while also learning how science has evolved throughout time.

Recent visitors say this is do-not-miss attraction, for kids but also for those young at heart, since there are interactive exhibits for all curious minds. Even if you don't have time to take a spin through the museum, past visitors said you should still go to access the free rooftop terrace, which offers panoramic views of the city and a cafe and does not charge an entrance fee.

Everyone ages 4 and older pays the same admission fee (16.50 euros, about $20) at NEMO; however, most visitors say their euros were well-spent. Kids, ages 3 and younger can enter for free. NEMO is open Tuesday through Sunday from 10 a.m. to 5:30 p.m., and on

Mondays from 10 a.m. to 5:30 p.m. February through September.

Oosterdok 2 1011 VX Amsterdam, Netherlands

Zandvoort

You probably knew about Amsterdam's canals, but what about its beach? Just about 20 miles west of the city center is a place called Zandvoort, a strip of sand that borders the North Sea. Experts say Zandvoort is at its best in the summertime, though recent visitors say a trip here in the offseason is also worthwhile since it lacks the summertime crowds.

Along with its wide shoreline, Zandvoort also boasts a variety of trendy beach clubs, including the popular Tijn Akersloot and Safari Lounge. When you've had your fill of the beach, explore the town a recommendation from past visitors.

You can take a 30-minute train ride directly from Amsterdam's Centraal station; during other seasons, you'll need to transfer (change at Haarlem for Zandvoort aan Zee).

Museum Het Rembrandthuis (Rembrandt House)

Rembrandt van Rijn (yep, Rembrandt is his first, not last name) once lived and worked in this restored home. So not only will you see the most complete collection of his etchings here, you'll also view his own interesting accumulation of objets d'art, from musical instruments to Roman busts. An audio guide is included in the admission, and many travelers recommend using it. Several travelers also highly recommend watching one of the etching demonstrations, which they say gives a more comprehensive understanding of the art and takes place three times a day. However, if you're traveling with kids, you may want to skip this attraction as past visitors said there is little to interest youngsters.

Keep in mind that there are no Rembrandt paintings only etchings much to the chagrin of some recent travelers, though there are paintings by Rembrandt's contemporaries, such as Pieter Lastman. The museum is open daily from 10 a.m. to 6 p.m., and charges 13 euros (about $16) for adult admission and 4 euros (about $5) for children ages 6 to 17 (visitors 5 and younger are admitted for free). If you purchased an I amsterdam card, your entry fee is waived. Visitors can take the 9 or 14 tram to the Waterlooplein stop.

Things NOT to Do in Amsterdam

Amsterdam has the reputation of being an "anything goes" city. Its relaxed, permissive, tolerant, liberal approach to things like sex and drugs are legendary, so one might think there were no rules or guidelines to abide by here. But, like anyplace, there are some dos and don'ts to keep in mind when visiting the Dutch capital. Plenty of guidebooks and Google searches can tell you the things to do and the sites to see. This list is a bit different. Here are 15 things NOT to do in Amsterdam.

1. Don't Take Pictures of the Women in the Windows

One of the most popular neighborhoods visitors flock to Amsterdam is De Wallen, the infamous Red Light District. As the oldest area in the city, it's full of historic architecture, scenic canals and cobblestone alleyways. But that's not what draws the tourist hordes. They're here to check out the 300-odd window parlors of prostitutes on display like wares at a farmer's market. Not everyone who comes to the RDL is looking to procure the produce, so to speak. Some just want to gawk at the salacious spectacle of it all. You'll see wolfpacks of drunken guys, curious couples, gaggles of hen partiers and camera toting Japanese bus tourists among the "interested shoppers". Look, even touch if you so desire (its not our place to judge), but do NOT take pictures of the working girls. That is strictly prohibited around here. If you get caught sneaking a pic, things could get confrontational.

2. Don't Mistake the Blue Lights in the Red Light District

It's no big shocker that De Wallen is known as the Red Light District, as the kamer sex cabins are literally illuminated with red lights. However, you may notice that a few of the windows are bathed in blue light. That indicates that a transgender sex worker is behind the glass. Not all buyers are aware of this, and some get a little more than they expect from their surprise encounter. However, if you're looking for a such an experience, go towards the blue light.

3. Don't Confuse Coffee Shops for a Starbucks

Amsterdam is famous for its coffee shops, but don't mistake these for cafes. If you want a cappuccino, find a sidewalk cafe to get your caffeine fix. The so-called coffee shops are for a fix of another kind. For those who don't know, cannabis, hash and other soft drugs are tolerated in these establishments. They don't sell alcohol, but some have food on the menu (and not just brownies). There are about 200 coffee shops in the city, and while they're not allowed to advertise, it's not hard to identify and locate one. Look for a green and white license sticker in the window. Be aware, the herbs might be more potent here than you're used to, so go easy on the stuff.

4. Don't Light up a Cigarette at a Coffee Shop

Some visitors are surprised to find that, while you can legally light up a joint in an Amsterdam coffee shop, you can't puff on a cigarette in public indoor spaces here. Weed, yes, but not tobacco. Some places turn a blind eye to this, and a few have designated smoking areas away from other patrons. However, many others enforce the anti-smoking rule with fines

5. Don't Think Drugs are Legal Here

A little clarification is in order in regards to Amsterdam's approach to drugs. Contrary to popular belief, recreational drugs are technically illegal here, pot included. The twist is that the Netherlands decriminalized possession of under 5 grams of cannabis back in 1976. This has led to a generally accepted tolerance on over 18s purchasing small quantities of the substance for personal use in coffee shops (see #3) and herbal "smart shops". Don't think you can just light a spliff and get stoned on the streets here. Note, also, that growing, processing and trading drugs is a criminal offense in the Netherlands. Furthermore, hard drugs like cocaine, LSD and heroin are also forbidden, and as of 2008, even magic mushrooms are banned. It's interesting to note that most of the cannabis consumption here is by foreign tourists. The local youth, who don't see it as forbidden fruit, generally don't find it all that appealing.

6. Don't Buy Drugs from Street Dealers

It should go without saying, but it's worth repeating because of Amsterdam's hedonistic reputation. Walk around the streets and you'll probably be approached by someone selling nefarious substances. Like anywhere, buying from them is just asking for trouble.

Drugs are bad for you (duh) but you'll have no idea what exactly you're getting off a random pusher. With other legally tolerated buzz options open to you in the coffee shops, there's no need to go rogue and buy questionable quality from an unregulated dealer, and risk turning your vacation into a really bad trip.

7. Don't Accept Cookies from Strangers

On a similar note, there's a known street scam where some friendly stranger will offer you a tempting cookie. Often it's a pretty Dutch girl, a cute young boy or a grandmotherly figure who charms you into thinking this is simply homespun Holland hospitality. However, the baked goodie contains some dodgy ingredients, and while you zone out in a stupor, your valuables are snatched. Similar scams like this happen all over the world, but this one's an Amsterdam special to be on guard for. Just follow mom's standard advice and don't accept candy or other treats from strangers.

8. Don't Pee in the Canals

Cringe that this even has to be mentioned, but you'd be surprised how many drunken/high tourist buffoons stagger through the Amsterdam streets at night and feel compelled to take a whiz in the pretty canals. Something about the water, perhaps? Have a little decorum, decency and bladder control, please, and refrain from relieving yourselves in this public historic waterway. Using this as your personal urinal is just not cool.

9. Don't Drive a Car

Compact Amsterdam is a pedestrian or pedal-pusher's paradise. You can get around to almost anywhere you want on foot or by bike, which is much more pleasant (and sustainable!) than being stuck behind a steering wheel. If you need to go a little further afield, public transportation is efficient and taxis are plentiful. There's no reason to rent a car to navigate the narrow 17th-century city streets, where parking, congestion and the canals will just confuse you. Besides, all those pedestrians, cyclists and trams make driving more stressful. Sure, use a car if you want to explore outside the city, but keep your vehicle in a Park and Ride carpark on the outskirts and plan on being car-free when in Amsterdam.

10. Don't Block the Bike Paths

A word to the wise for pedestrians and tourists on rental bikes. Beware the steady stream of cyclists who own the lanes on most city streets. Don't stop to take a selfie, check a map or gawk at the scenic canal in the middle of the bike flow, or you're asking for an altercation with a local. With 500 kms of bike paths in the Dutch capital, two-wheeled transportation is a great way to go here, but know the etiquette and rules of the road before saddling up or strolling within their midst.

11. Don't Cycle at Night Without Lights

If you do choose to cycle in Amsterdam, don't forget to light up at night. Yes, you'll see locals breaking this rule all the time. However, it is technically required by law to use front and back lights on your bike after dark.

Besides, it's just common sense to want to see where you're going and have others see you, too.

12. Don't Rent a MacBike or You'll Flag Yourself as a Tourist

One of the oldest and most popular rental bike companies in Amsterdam is MacBike. They offer guided tours as well as a variety of bicycles and accessories to rent from five central locations. Nothing against this fine company, per se, but as their distinctive red bikes come with a big circular logo on them, you will be essentially flagging yourself as a pedalling tourist. Same goes for the Yellow Bike company. Not to fuel paranoia, but this could make you a bit of a target for those that like to prey on unsuspecting visitors. There are other bike rental companies in town where you can blend in with the locals a bit better

13. Don't Drink Heineken

We have nothing against this pleasant pale lager in the signature green bottle. In fact, we encourage you to visit the Heineken Experience when in Amsterdam to learn about the brew. However, this premium beer brand has done a great job marketing and exporting itself around the world and you can probably enjoy it back home any time you choose. Ditto for Amstel, Grolsch and Bavaria. There are many amazing local beers from microbreweries to sample in the city pubs. Beer connoisseurs should check out 't Arendsnest, De Brabantse Aap, Brouwerij 't IJ or de Prael for some local craft beer flavors.

14. Don't Line Up for Anne Frank's House

One of the must-see sites of Amsterdam is, of course, the house where Anne Frank and her family hid out in a secret annex for two years during WWII. With the popularity of her famous diary, the line ups at the museum can reach epic proportions, especially during the high summer season. We're all for spontaneous, serendipitous tourism and not being locked into set itineraries, but this is one attraction to plan ahead for or else you could suck away 2 to 4 hours waiting in a line (and perhaps not even get in). You can easily pre-book a timed ticket online to get direct entrance at a door beside the main entry point. Do this as far in advance as you can, as a limited number are available each day.

15. Don't Miss the Poffertjes

Another one of the things not to do in Amsterdam is to miss an opportunity to eat *poffertjes*. These spongy spheres are kind of like a Dutch donut hole (but better). The sugar-dusted pancake puffs are available from street vendors and markets around Amsterdam, served with a knob of butter and optional toppings like Nutella or strawberries but we prefer plain. There are many other delicious Dutch delicacies to indulge in when in Amsterdam. Cheese, herring, *bitterballen* and *stroopwafel* spring to mind. But *poffertje* balls of bliss are an addictive treat you shouldn't even try to resist. Betcha can't eat just one.

Things You Need to Know Before Visiting

Amsterdam travel tips to make your trip a little more affordable.

How can anyone not like Amsterdam? There are pretty canals, narrow houses, cute bridges, plenty of bicycles, flowers everywhere and an extremely liberal culture. It's the city that's gateway to Europe for many 20 and 30 something travelers who start their Euro trips here.

Yes, Amsterdam is absolutely gorgeous and you will not be able to stop yourself from clicking hundreds of photos while you're there. But it's not Amsterdam's beauty that WOWs me, it is the fact that literally every kind of traveler will find something fun to do here is what makes it special. Wether you're traveling to Amsterdam alone or with your family, you will surely enjoy your time here.

I visited Amsterdam for the first time back in 2014 but one visit was not enough. I visited this glorious city just a few days back and I can't stop thinking about it. In fact, I'd love to visit it again in autumn and then again during the winter months.

If you're visiting Europe anytime soon, please do yourself a favor and include Amsterdam in your itinerary. However, keep in mind that Amsterdam can end up being super expensive if you don't research enough. Based on my experience, I want to share my top travel tips for Amsterdam with you so that you can save some money while you're there. Wether you're visiting Amsterdam for the first time or the third time, some of these tips are sure to help you while you're there

Avoid Weekends and Visit during the week = Cheaper Rooms

Amsterdam is one of the most visited destinations of Europe and over 7 million international travelers visit Amsterdam in a year. Many Europeans who live in nearby cities frequently visit Amsterdam over a long weekend. This happens even more during summer months.

Believe it or not, but a dorm bed that costs $20 during the week, can be as high as $70 or $80 during the weekend. If you plan well in advance and research, you can save some serious money by just making sure you visit Amsterdam on any of the weekdays. Moreover, you will save a lot of time when you don't have to stand in long queues and can ultimately explore more.

Get yourself an I Amsterdam Card

Apart from your accommodation costs, where do you think you will spend most of your money while you're in Amsterdam? I'm sure you're thinking internal local transport, boat ride, museum entry, food, etc. Well, good news you can save money on this by getting yourself an I Amsterdam city card.

Based on your duration of stay, you can get yourself a card that is valid for 1 to 4 days. A 24-hour card is for 59 euros and a 4-day card is for 98 euros. This card includes a free entry to most of the top museums in Amsterdam, unlimited use of public transport (trams, buses and metros), free canal cruise, and discounts in many restaurants.

I Amsterdam card is a blessing and I wish I had it back in 2014 when I first visited this city. The best part is that, the transport parts and museum parts of this cards get activated separately. The museums part is automatically activated when you visit a museum the first time, and stays active till the duration of your card.

The public transport part of the I Amsterdam card is automatically activated the first time you use a tram, bus or metro in Amsterdam. This way, you don't have to get a card for the full duration of your trip and can just plan your trip in such a way that you check out all the museums in a day or two, overlap one day with transport and include museums which you can't reach by walking and extend the card longer.

In short: if you're visiting Amsterdam for the first time for a quick visit and want to visit all the major attractions, this I Amsterdam card will save you a lot of time and money.

Coffeeshops in Amsterdam are not exactly Cafes

A coffeeshop in Amsterdam is not your typical café but means something else entirely. I feel it is my duty to educate you so that you don't get a shock when you visit a coffeeshop in Amsterdam just to drink coffee.

I'm sure you know by know that Amsterdam is one of those few places on earth where you can legally buy and consume marijuana for personal use. This happens not on the streets but in coffeeshops where you can see several kinds of weed, hash, etc., being sold per gram or in pre rolled joints.

Check point 8 for Amsterdam tips for stoners, more information about coffee shops and safety while experimenting / buying drugs in Amsterdam

No Photography in the Red Light District

Yes, prostitution is legal in Amsterdam and the red light district comes alive as soon as the evening sets in.

If you walk around the red light district at night, you will see prostitutes through pretty much every glass window in this area.

If you're visiting Amsterdam's Red Light District just to look around, please don't photograph the sex workers that you see through the windows. Just because they're sex workers, doesn't mean you can disrespect them. Not only clicking these photographs is rude but you can get your camera snatched by the cops or pay a hefty fine. Believe it or not, I saw many people who were trying to photograph the prostitutes and were caught by the cops.

Don't Get in the way of cyclists

One of the first things that you will notice about Amsterdam is its bicycle dominated roads. The city is full of them and the locals love traveling on them. After all, Amsterdam has been declared as the most bicycle friendly city in the world. As per the Amsterdam tourism board website, there are more bikes in Amsterdam than permanent residents!

However, much to annoyance of the locals, many tourists don't notice the bike lanes and walk on them. A bike obviously doesn't move like a car, and it is not easy to stop it instantly within seconds. Please be mindful of bike lanes and stay off them to avoid getting injured.

If you love cycling, then I highly recommend you to explore Amsterdam on a bicycle. San and I carried own bicycles from Germany on a train to Amsterdam and cycled around the city. You don't really have to carry your own bicycle like we did, but you can book one of the many tours. Here are some of them:

It can rain anytime in Amsterdam, so be prepared

Not just London, but it can rain anytime in Amsterdam too. Prepare yourself mentally and physically to handle the rain. If you want to be comfortable, don't forget to carry your rain gear, especially shoes. Carry gumboots or flip flops, or any other rainproof shoes so that your socks don't get soggy.

If you forget to carry your rain poncho, don't worry because you will find cheap rain ponchos being sold for 1 5 euros in several stores.

Carry a bottle and drink tap water

The Netherlands is one such country where the quality of tap water is regulated and is totally safe to drink it. A water bottle can cost around 2 euros and you can save some money by filling your bottle with tap water. Why waste money on bottled water when you can safely drink tap water?

If you think bottled water is cleaner, let me tell you it depends on how it is stored and transported. These bottles are made with plastic and if they're kept in the sun by mistake for a long duration, the water is no longer safe. Before you proceed, here's a 10 second long video with a 360 degree view of Amsterdam.

Amsterdam tips for Stoners Don't buy drugs on the road

Ok, so you have heard Amsterdam has an open-minded drug use policy and you are visiting this city just to party. I understand, but please don't buy drugs on the road. Believe it or not, there are cops everywhere and you can get caught. Why buy on the road when you can legally buy and smoke weed (and hash) in coffeeshops? In Bulldog (Amsterdam's most famous coffeeshop), a gram of weed or hash is sold for around 10 12 euros. You can also buy 4 pre rolled splifs for around 16 euros. By the way, if you're a first time smoker in Amsterdam then I feel it's my duty to warn you go SLOW.

As of 2008, you can no longer buy magic mushrooms in Amsterdam but can buy truffles in head shops (or smart shops). Truffles are just like magic mushrooms, except they grow under the earth. There is a herbal version of many things, including MDMA. Just because it is herbal, doesn't mean it doesn't cause any damage to your body. Please research well in advance before you decide to experiment here.

Park your car outside Amsterdam

Parking in Amsterdam is expensive and can be as high as 10 euro per hour. If you're reaching Amsterdam by driving, then you need to park your car outside to save money.

On the highway that leads to Amsterdam, watch out for "P+R" signs because this is where you need to park your car. Parking in P+R spots is usually 1 euro per hour and from here you can easily take public transport to the centre of the city.

Don't Get Stuck at the Centre. Get out and explore

Amsterdam is more than just coffeeshops, red light district and the center. Many tourists just get stuck in the center and miss the surrounding neighborhoods.

Spend a few days in the city's hipster neighborhood Amsterdam-Noord and get lost in NDSM. Go visit the nearby Jordaan, or Oost you will be surprised to see how few tourists visit these places. You can easily reach here by hopping on trams, buses and metros where you can use your I Amsterdam city card.

You will probably get lost

Prepare to get lost because in the beginning, most of the canals in Amsterdam will look similar and you will think you're walking in circles. Some streets are so narrow that it is very easy to miss a turn. Moreover, if you rent a bike, the traffic can be confusing because there are trams, buses, cars and pedestrians on the road.

I am not sure about you but I really enjoy getting lost in new places. However, it is not so much fun when you get lost right before you need to catch a train (or bus in my case) to get out of Amsterdam. Download an offline version of Amsterdam's map on Google maps or Maps me, so that you can be aware of where you are.

Respect the locals and their city

Just because Amsterdam's city council is open-minded and has legalized many things like marijuana consumption, prostitution, etc., it doesn't mean that you can take advantage of this. Be a responsible traveler and don't do more than you can handle.

Don't get excessively high in public places and please don't create a scene. Prostitutes are not porn stars, don't photograph them and share their pictures on social media. Just remember to treat Amsterdam exactly how you would want the visitors to treat YOUR hometown.

Carry your photo ID

No, you don't just need a photo ID if you're visiting a coffeeshop or a bar, but even the cops can stop you on the road and ask for an ID. We were told this happens specifically when people look intoxicated or have "red eyes".

You may just be sleepy but perhaps you look stoned, it is better to keep your ID with you all the time. If you're worried about losing your passport, then just keep your driver's license that shows your picture.

Amsterdam has pickpockets, beware

Just like most touristy places, Amsterdam also has pickpockets. Moreover, some of the areas tend to get highly crowded and you may not even notice when someone picks your pockets. Keep your valuables in your hotel room or hostel locker and carry only the essentials.

Where to stay in Amsterdam

Amsterdam is one of those places where you need to book a room in advance to avoid shockingly high costs. Believe it or not, my husband once paid 20 euros for just two hours in a hostel, which is usually a nightly cost in hostels all over Europe.

The best insider's tips to Amsterdam

Amsterdam's reputation for stag dos, spliff and sex tourism belies the rich pickings beyond Dam Square. Described by locals as a village, Amsterdam has the arts, entertainment and startup scene of many larger cities but retains a friendly and relaxed atmosphere. As a resident, I love that all my favourite places are just a short journey away. The vibe is laid-back and the dress code avoids the stiff chic of more status-conscious cities: the rule is, if you can't cycle in it, don't wear it. From picturesque narrow streets of higgledy-piggledy houses to sweaty techno nights in converted factories, this city reveals its many faces to those willing to stray from the tourist hotspots.

Gs Brunch Boat

The best way to explore Amsterdam is from the water. Gs Brunch Boat, a converted coal barge with a retro interior and sunshine roof, offers a cosy alternative to the regular tour boat formulas. The €39.50 cover price includes the boat trip and à la carte menu, including eggs Benedict and bloody marys. The round trip lasts 1¾ hours and passes through the historical centre for some gable-gazing and out to the IJ harbour with its modern architecture.

Boards by Keizersgracht 177. Sails Sat-Sun in winter and Fri-Sun from April to August. Departure times vary

Ons' Lieve Heer Op Solder

The Anne Frank House is not the only secret attic in Amsterdam worth visiting. In the heart of the busy red light district is a 17th-century Catholic church constructed in the attic of a merchant's house during the Protestant reformation. An audio guide tells the story of the church and takes you on a historical tour of the building, describing how its owners once lived. An abundance of iconographic art and interesting artefacts satisfy the curiosity, while the Voices of Tolerance exhibition promotes a wider reflection on religious freedom. Lacking the queues of the Anne Frank House and the Rijksmuseum the city's only museum older than it Op Solder is a great alternative to the usual tourist tick-list and a splendid example of Dutch Golden Age architecture.

Adult €11, child €5.50, open Mon-Sat 10am-6pm, Sun 1pm-6pm, Oudezijds Voorburgwal 38

Huis Marseille

The predominantly modern works in this photography gallery are in contrast to the 17th-century buildings in which they hang. Attracting talent from around the world, such as Dana Lixenberg and Jamie Hawkesworth, Huis Marseille's exhibitions broach a range of challenging themes, from the personal to the political. The ornamental garden behind the museum is a quiet space to escape the city but if it's boutiques and bars you want, explore the Negen Straatjes, nine cute shopping streets that cut through the central canals.

Entrance €8, under-17s free, open 11am-6pm, closed Monday. Keizersgracht 399-401,

Restaurant De Struisvogel

Distracted by the beautifully-lit bridges and chocolate-box buildings of the Keizersgracht canal, it would be easy to miss one of its treasures as the door to Restaurant De Struisvogel (The Ostrich) is below eye level and leads into a basement. Inside, wooden furniture and a giant chalkboard of choices at sensible prices create an unpretentious dining atmosphere. The three-course set menu is €28.50 and includes simple starters paté, salad or soup followed by mains such as ostrich steak with a quince compote (€4.50 supplement) and haddock with red pepper, fennel and mussels. There are just two sittings, so booking is essential. If it's full, try its new sister restaurant Bistro De Struisvogel, a five-minute walk away.

Open Sun-Fri from 5.30pm, Sat from 5pm. Keizersgacht 312,

Pllek

The 14-minute ferry trip from Centraal Station to NDSM wharf is free and opens up a world of urban cool in Amsterdam Noord. One of the jewels in this landscape of shipping containers and warehouses is Pllek, a beach bar and music venue a short walk from the drop-off point. The corrugated metal structure and galleried seating works with the leather sofas, picnic benches and school desks. The programme is eclectic, with live music, dance, yoga, and film, as well as all-day food. Expect a festival-like atmosphere in the summer, when bonfires are lit and revellers and music acts spill out onto the beach in a happy muddle.

Opening times vary until late in summer, TT Neveritaweg 59

Westerpark

If you head north-west on the lively Haarlemmerstraat, past its cool coffee shops and stores, you eventually arrive at the Westerpark. Less busy than the famous Vondelpark to the south, this park is about playgrounds and dog-walkers in the day and culture and clubbing at night, as the Westergasfabriek a former gasworks comes to life. Try the Bakkerswinkel for breakfast for around €10. Lunch is sandwiches or soup from €6, or salads from €9. The cafe also serves high tea from €17.50pp. Grab some Dutch ice-cream at nearby Ijscuypje or a chunky bar of Dutch chocolate at Tony's Chocolonely where fun flavours include orange and rosemary and milk popcorn discodip.

Albert Cuyp market

This lively street market in the Pijp district, south of the centre, is over 100 years old and claims to be the largest daily market in Europe. Fruit and veg, fish, flowers and clothes are the staples but the list goes on. For sampling cheese, poffertjes (tiny pancakes) or herring at local prices, this is a great place to start. The Pijp is full of fun spots to drink and dine once the market is closed. Check out nearby Pho 91 for tangy Vietnamese soup and then head south to Brouwerij Troost, a former monastery serving beer brewed on site.

Open Mon-Sat 9am-5pm, Albert Cuypstraat

Mr Blou I Love You

The owner of Mr Blou ... is a former Michelin-starred chef who wanted more contact with people and, believing that everybody should eat well, whatever their means, he opened his food stall in October 2017. The focus is on vegan street food but there is chicken, too. Around 95% of the produce is organic and most is locally sourced, including Lot Sixty One coffee, which is roasted less than 10 minutes' walk away at Kinkerstraat 112. There are cakes, smoothies, wraps and salads but the homemade falafel takes centre stage. Lunch and a drink is around €11. Curl up on the sheepskin-covered benches under the awnings or eat your take-out while exploring the pretty streets in the nearby Jordaan district.

Open Mon-Sat, 11am-8pm in winter and 9am-10pm in summer

OT301

This former squat is full of artistic activity, much of it free of charge. Resident artists and community classes occupy the centre by day, while evenings mean films, live music, DJs and jam sessions. The bar on the left is the main hub and is home to De Peper, where volunteers serve pay-what-you-can vegan food four days a week (7pm-8.30pm). In a back room is the table tennis bar (Tuesdays) and, hidden in the basement, a radio station plays juicy beats to an internet audience. The air smells damp, but the sound is wonderful.

Opening times vary.

The Tire Station

There's trendy accommodation at an affordable price at this 112-bedroom hotel, which prides itself on its environmental credentials but refuses to be preachy and even has parking a rarity in Amsterdam. Inside this former Michelin tyre station, the design is modern, industrial and angular, with exposed piping and a sand-cement floor. Upstairs, the pinboard feature wall, cheeky word art, and the minimalist decor of the bedrooms, create a relaxed, studenty feel, while the Royal Dutch Auping beds help with a good night's sleep. The hotel is close to the 120-acre Vondelpark and a 10-minute tram ride from the centre. When you have tried out the hotel's own cafe and restaurant, continue down Amstelveenseweg for a huge choice of bars and restaurants to suit all budgets.

Rooms from €80 room-only in low season, organic breakfast €15,

Getting there
The new Eurostar route from London to Amsterdam starts on 4 April but tickets go on sale on 20 February.

Fares will start from £35 each way and the outward journey will take 3 hours 41 minutes, the return leg (with a change in Brussels) around an hour longer. There are direct flights to Amsterdam Schiphol from 26 UK airports, starting at around £47 return, carriers include Aer Lingus, BA, CityJet, easyJet, Eurowings, Flybe, Jet2, KLM and Vueling.

Best time to go
27 April for Koningsdag (King's Day), the all-orange, all-day street party in celebration of King Willem-Alexander's birthday. 15-17 June for Open Garden Weekend, when many of the grand courtyards concealed behind the canal houses are opened up to the public. 4 August for the Canal Parade, the highlight of Pride Amsterdam, when the whole town comes out to cheer on the elaborate floats and their costumed LGBTQ crew.

Exchange rate £1 = €1.13; a small draft beer (25cl) costs about €3

Since you're here…………

… we have a small favour to ask. More people are reading the Guardian than ever but advertising revenues across the media are falling fast. And unlike many news organisations, we haven't put up a paywall we want to keep our journalism as open as we can. So you can see why we need to ask for your help.

The Guardian is editorially independent, meaning we set our own agenda. Our journalism is free from commercial bias and not influenced by billionaire owners, politicians or shareholders. No one edits our editor. No one steers our opinion. This is important because it enables us to give a voice to the voiceless, challenge the powerful and hold them to account. It's what makes us different to so many others in the media, at a time when factual, honest reporting is critical.

Best Times to Visit Amsterdam

The best time to visit Amsterdam is between April and May or September and November right before or directly after the summertime high tourist season. You'll contend with fewer tourists, you'll enjoy somewhat mild temperatures (the city's weather is notoriously finicky), and you'll also experience Amsterdam as the locals do at its laid-back best. But if it's a deal you're after and you don't mind temperatures in the 30 to 40-degree range you should plan a winter vacation; you'll find lower hotel rates and depleted crowds at the city's top sites. No matter what time of year you plan to visit, you'll find the city offers a jampacked social calendar (it hosts more than 300 festivals a year).

June-August

With average highs in the low 70s and long sunny days, it takes no leap of the imagination to see why Amsterdam is so popular in the summertime. But along with hospitable weather, Amsterdam fills with tourists packing the popular sites. Hotels are also at a premium and unless you book far in advance largely without a vacancy.

Key Events:

> ➤ Holland Festival (June-July)

> ➤ Taste of Amsterdam (June)

> ➤ Amsterdam Gay Pride (July-August)

> ➤ Grachtenfestival(August)

> ➤ Jordaan Festival (August)

September-November

Fewer crowds and relatively mild weather (with highs in the 50s and 60s) makes fall a pleasant season for travel. You might be able to score slight breaks on hotel prices, but you may or may not miss out on the cold weather, so plan to pack layers and an umbrella.

Key Events:

> ➤ UNESCO World Heritage Weekend (September)

> ➤ Amsterdam Fringe Festival (September)

> ➤ TCS Amsterdam Marathon (October)

> ➤ Amsterdam Light Festival (November-January)

December-March

Short, dark and nearly freezing days make winter in Amsterdam pretty unpleasant. But this chilly time of year temperatures fluctuate between 30 and 40 degrees Fahrenheit is also the best time to score deals on airfare and hotel rooms. If you do brave the cold, don't forget a warm coat and maybe a pair of thermal underwear or two. For more favorable weather, plan to visit in mid- to late March.

Key Events:

> ➤ Amsterdam Light Festival (November-January)

> ➤ New Year's Eve (December 31)

> ➤ National Tulip Day (January)

> ➤ Keukenhof Flower Garden (March-May)

April-May

With temperatures on the rise and tulips in bloom, spring is a nice time to visit. To see the city's notorious tulips at their peak, visit during the last two weeks of April and the first two weeks of May.

Key Events:

- ➢ Keukenhof Flower Garden (March-May)

- ➢ National Restaurant Week (April)

- ➢ King's Day (April)

- ➢ Tulip Festival (April)

- ➢ Liberation Day (May)

How to Save Money in Amsterdam

Purchase an "I amsterdam City Card" This little piece of plastic grants you free, unlimited use of GVB public transportation, free access to dozens of museums and a complimentary canal cruise, among other perks, for a set price. The catch? You buy your card for 24, 48, 72 or 96 hours and can only access the deals within those time periods.

Do the heel-toe step Walking rather than taking taxis or public transportation will cut down on costs. And this small city is immensely walkable; just leave a wide berth between you and the serious cyclists using the bike lanes.

Visit in winter Invest in a cozy coat and come to Amsterdam in the winter, where the discounted hotel rates will keep you feeling warm and fuzzy. An added bonus: crowds are at an all-time low, as are lines for top attractions.

What to Eat

From raw herring to pancakes and rice tables too Amsterdam, like many other international cities, is filled with a multiplicity of national and international cuisines. Take its Dutch pancakes, which come smothered or stuffed with every topping imaginable, from bacon to blueberries. (Recent travelers rave about The Pancake Bakery). Raw herring is another Netherlands specialty and is consumed whole. Jenever, or Dutch gin, is another must-try, and one of the loveliest places to enjoy it might be the idyllic Distillery 't Nieuwe Diep.

Indonesian rijsttafel (or rice tables) rice topped with spiced meats, vegetables and fish are hugely popular. For some of the best, try Restaurant Blauw, Sampurna or Restaurant Jun. Indonesian establishments are scattered throughout the city. Cheap ethnic eats are mainly gathered in the De Pijp neighborhood.

For an upscale dining experience, try the Negen Straatjes (The Nine Streets) or the Reguliersdwarsstraat areas. Travelers also praise the food finds on Elandsgracht Street in the Canal Ring. Beware tourist traps in the party-hearty areas of Rembrandtplein, Leidseplein and the Red Light District

Safety

Although the Netherlands government takes a lax look at prostitution in the Red Light District and marijuana use at the coffeehouses throughout the city, travelers should be careful. Visitors, especially women, should be wary of wandering around the Red Light District in the evening alone, as the area tends to attract unruly groups of men. Possession of marijuana and definitely the possession/use of other drugs, such as heroin and cocaine, can get you into a lot of trouble with the authorities. And before you visit, you might want to follow local news for the latest updates on rules and regulations.

Getting Around Amsterdam

The best way to get around Amsterdam is by bike. Once you've flown into the nearby Amsterdam Airport Schiphol (AMS) and settled into your hotel, we suggest you inquire about getting your own two wheels. Numerous canals, impatient drivers and narrow roads (ringing the Canal Belt) make maneuvering the city via car interesting, to say the least. Plus, Amsterdam is known for its biking, and you'll find that rental shops canvas the city. Pedaling through an unfamiliar place might not be for everyone, though; for those travelers, there's also a perfectly respectable public transport system the GVB which offers metro, bus and tram service. And if you purchased an I amsterdam City Card, all your rides on public transportation are covered.

From the airport, you can reach the city center via bus, train or taxi. Taxi fares from the airport to the city center typically cost 40 to 60 euros (about $50 to $75). Travelers are advised not to take rides from drivers soliciting within the airport; instead, find the taxi rank at the airport's exit. This is where officially approved taxi drivers congregate.

Car

Getting around Amsterdam by car probably isn't the best method. If you do decide to drive, frustration and expense will no doubt be your companions. Along with narrow, one-way roads, scarce parking that's expensive to boot and multitudes of pedestrians and cyclists on all sides, you also have a disorienting tangle of canals to grapple with. However, if you're planning on seeing other destinations outside of the city, renting a car does make a bit more sense. You can find rental places at the airport, as well as a throughout downtown. For tourists, the most important road to know is the A10, which makes a loop around the city. Intersecting the road are 18 S-routes, which offer direct paths into different districts of the city. Keep in mind that most rental agencies require drivers to be at least 21, or even 25 in some cases, but a valid U.S. driver's license will suffice.

Bus

Amsterdam's public bus service, which offers 42 bus routes, is operated by GVB. Many of the buses begin their routes at Centraal Station, which is also one of the places where you can buy your GVB *OV-chipkaart, the public transport card that is used for trams and metros as well as buses*. The most convenient option for travelers tends to be either a one-hour ticket, which is good for travel within one hour, or the day card, which can be purchased for one day or up to seven days. Although one-hour cards can be purchased aboard buses, visitors will have to purchase day cards at ticket vending machines at metro stops, or at the airport, among other places. One-day passes start at 7.50 euros (a little more than $9); one-hour passes cost 3 euros (less than $4). The GVB also operates night buses on 12 routes, but ticket prices for these are more expensive than their daytime counterparts. Top sites, such as the NEMO Science **Museum**, can be reached by bus; Nos. 22 and 48 make stops there.

Metro

Amsterdam also operates a small metro system, with four numbered lines: 50, 51, 53 and 54. Metro trains are mostly used by residents coming in from the suburbs, but travelers are welcome to use them too with their GVB OV-chipkaart, which can also be used on the metro and tram. If you do decide to take the metro train, be sure to validate your ticket on the platform before hopping on.

Tram

After walking or biking, the Amsterdam tram is the most scenic way to travel through the city. Fifteen tram routes crisscross the city, and visitors can use their GVB OV-chipkaart to take a ride on the 200-some trams offered. As with the bus or the metro, the most convenient ticket option on the tram is either a one-hour ticket or the day card, which can be purchased for one day or up to seven days. When boarding the tram, visitors should enter toward the front; to hop out, they can head to the rear and hit the green button on or next to the door. Top sights, such as the Anne Frank House, can be reached by tram; Nos. 13, 14 and 17 all make stops there.

Ferry

To get across the IJ river, you can take one of seven free ferry routes operated by the GVB. Although you might enjoy a scenic view of the harbor, there's not a ton to do once you reach Amsterdam-Noord (North), though the area is currently undergoing a revitalization. One of the more popular routes takes travelers between Amsterdam Central Station to Buiksloterweg, which is home to attractions like EYE Filmmuseum and Tolhuistuin.

Taxi and Water Taxi

Metered taxis can be hailed on the street, called or picked up at taxi stands. However, in recent years, taxi service has become a little iffy with directionally challenged cabbies, who may or may not speak English. Taxi Centrale Amsterdam tends to offer trustworthy service. Water taxis in Amsterdam are very expensive, but they're also a scenic way to see the city. Uber also operates in Amsterdam.

Bike

Biking is *the* way to travel around Amsterdam. In fact according to the 2017 Copenhagenize Index of the world's most bike-friendly cities, Amsterdam is among the top three behind Copenhagen and Utrecht (another Netherlands city). You'll be able to find bike rental shops throughout the city. MacBike, Yellow Bike and Damstraat Rent a Bike rank highly among past visitors. Prices vary by company, but you can expect to pay about 10 euros (around $12) for a half-day rental and less than 15 euros (approximately $18) for a full-day rental. If you're nervous about traffic, pedal around on Sunday when the city is sleepy. Bike tours are equally popular, especially those offered by Mike's Bike Tours Amsterdam.

Entry & Exit Requirements

A valid travel document is required for United States citizens entering the Netherlands by air or sea, as well as for U.S. citizens trying to re-enter the country. A passport is the preferred form of documentation, and children must have them, too. Passports must be valid for at least six months beyond planned date of departure and have at least two blank pages available for stamps. U.S. citizens do not need a visa unless they plan on staying longer than 90 days. Visit the U.S. State

Department's website for the latest information on foreign exit and entry requirements

10 Things to do in Amsterdam

It's one of the most popular tourist destinations in the world so much so that there is currently no marketing budget for the Netherlands capital city. It simply doesn't need it; visitors still arrive by the plane-load.

It's easy to see why. Amsterdam provides the perfect blend of history and culture to balance out the more risqué recreational pursuits offered by the Red Light District and plentiful "coffee" shops. As well as a myriad of flight options taking just over an hour, from December 2017 there are even more options

for Brits to get there as Eurostar launches its new direct train service from London St Pancras, taking around three hours and 50 minutes.

Get on yer bike

Amsterdam is a city of cyclists and there is no better way to discover the sights. It's also incredibly quick to get around on two wheels, making Amsterdam's already compact size infinitely easier to explore. Plenty of places hire out bikes and locks expect to pay around €35 for three days. Bike City (bikecity.nl) rents single speed, three-speed and seven-speed varieties, with the added bonus that they come in unobtrusive black more gaudy-coloured bikes that have obviously been hired can attract more attention from thieves

Once on your faithful steed, you can cycle pretty much anywhere alongside Amsterdam's famous canals, or head to Vondelpark, a beautiful park to the south-east of the city centre with a playground, ponds, open-air theatre and several giant sculptures, including The Fish by Picasso.

Soak up some art

Head to Museum Square in the Amsterdam South borough for more culture than you can shake a paintbrush at. The Rijksmuseum (rijksmuseum.nl) is one of the city's biggest draws, packed with masterpieces from Vermeer, Rembrandt et al. Allow yourself plenty of time to fully enjoy the many exhibitions on offer. Opening hours are 9am-5pm daily and entry costs €17.50; it's far preferable to book online in advance and avoid the queues.

Meanwhile, head next door to the Van Gogh Museum (vangoghmuseum.nl) for the world's largest collection of Van Gogh pieces. A wander through the fascinating rooms charts how the master's work developed throughout his life. Open Sunday to Thursday from 9am-7pm, Friday 9am-10pm, Saturday 9am-9pm; entry costs €17.

Eat like a local

Amsterdam, like any city worth its salt, has its fair share of fine dining places but the must-try dish can be picked up at less high-flying establishments. No trip is complete without sampling rijsttafel, which literally translates as "rice table". It's Indonesian in origin but was adapted by Dutch colonialists, who brought it back to the Netherlands in 1945 when Indonesia gained its independence. Rijsttafel consists of a huge number of small side dishes, including satay, pickles and egg rolls, accompanied by rice prepared in different ways. You can pick some up in any of the many Indonesian restaurants one of the best and most affordable is Tujuh Maret (tujuhmaret.nl), where you can pick up a set menu for €27.75.

Visit Anne Frank's house

Anne Frank and her famous diary have featured so much in films and television you might feel like you've been to her house before. But even being overly familiar with the story doesn't stop a visit to the place where Anne and her family hid for so long from the Nazis being indescribably moving. The journey takes you from the ground floor up many steep flights of stairs to the secret annex where they lived for over two years Anne's room has been preserved with pictures of movie stars and magazine clippings adorning the walls. Most emotive, perhaps, is the range of videos at the end of the tour, showing real-life scenes from concentration camps. It's all been extremely sensitively done, though you may leave feeling rather subdued. Booking online in advance is recommended (annefrank.org). Open daily 9am-10pm; entry costs €9.50.

Roll a joint

If you feel so inclined, Amsterdam's famously accepting attitude to drugs makes it an ideal place to experiment. If you're new to the game, steer clear of trying cannabis in any kind of baked good brownies and spacecakes are often very strong, and it's difficult to gauge when you've had too much. Instead, head to one of the city's coffee shops and start off light with a pre-rolled joint or choose your poison and roll your own. Share with friends, along with an actual coffee, if you like, and let the good vibes roll. Dampkring (dampkring-coffeeshop-amsterdam.nl) is known for having the most extensive menu in town, and frequently wins the Cannabis Cup. Smoothies, hot drinks and toasted sandwiches are also available.

Hop on a pedalo

Getting on the water is a must. There are countless boat trips doing laps of the many canals, but an even more fun way to explore is on a pedalo. There are several routes to choose from which take different amounts of time you'll usually be given a map to help with navigation. *Stromma (stromma.nl) hires out pedalos from three different locations, charging €12 for an* hour and a half.

Enjoy the Gezelligheid

The Dutch have a word for conviviality that warm, relaxed feeling when everything is just right with the world. Gezelligheid goes hand in hand with Amsterdam's many bruin cafés, or brown cafés. There are more than 1,000 of these old traditional pubs in Amsterdam, named after their wood panels and tobacco-stained wallpaper. They're wonderful places to sit, drink, and enjoy deep conversations over a locally brewed beer. Café Hoppe (cafehoppe.com), located on a central square a few minutes from Amsterdam's flower market, epitomises the genre, with rough stone floors, wood-panelled walls, an impressive number of beers on tap and a selection of deep-fried snacks.

Surround yourself with cats

One of Amsterdam's most delightfully odd attractions is a museum called Kattenkabinet (kattenkabinet.nl) essentially a house crammed with artworks that include, you guessed it, cats. Founded by a wealthy banker, Bob Meijer, in honour of his dearly departed tomcat John Pierpont Morgan, the collection includes a small Rembrandt and a Picasso, alongside a bizarre yet moving shrine to Meijer's favourite feline. But the best part of this off-beat museum is that real live cats can be found all over the place, lounging on tables and floors, and are very open to being stroked. Open 10am-4pm Monday to Friday, 12-5pm Saturday and Sunday; entry costs €6.

Put on the red light

Whether or not you agree with the Netherlands' legalisation of prostitution, having a look around Amsterdam's Red Light District in the city's medieval centre is a fascinating experience. There are countless half-naked girls behind windows, although it's not always as titillating as you might imagine; they mostly look bored while playing on their phones. For frank information about the whole business, head to the Prostitute Information Centre (pic-amsterdam.com), from where you can also catch an informative hour-long tour of the area. Tours are every Saturday at 5pm and cost €15.

Hit the shops

Amsterdam has a multitude of opportunities for retail therapy outdoor markets abound, selling everything from food to flowers, art to antiques. For fresh blooms, check out the Bloemenmarkt; for everything else, try the Albert Cuypmarkt (albertcuyp-markt.amsterdam). Here, Indonesian immigrants mix with locals, offering stall upon stall of bric-a-brac and delicious Dutch snacks. Nine Streets (theninestreets.com), meanwhile, has a plethora of boutique shops selling all kinds of quirky, one-off brands

The End

Lightning Source UK Ltd.
Milton Keynes UK
UKHW020634190521
383988UK00011B/653